Richard Demarco: | The Italian Connection

Richard Demarco | The Italian Connection wishes to thank its funders and sponsors:

RICHARD DEMARCO
THE ITALIAN CONNECTION

Arts and
Humanities
Research Council

Duncan of Jordanstone
College of Art & Design.
University of Dundee

ISTITUTO
italiano
DI CULTURA
EDIMBURGO

ING. ANTONIO
BUONO S.R.L.
IMPRESA DI COSTRUZIONI

Richard Demarco |
The Italian Connection

Edited by

Laura Leuzzi, Elaine Shemilt and Stephen Partridge

British Library Cataloguing in Publication Data

Richard Demarco |
The Italian Connection

A catalogue entry for this book is available from the British Library

ISBN: 9780 86196 753 7

Electronic editions:
EPUB: ISBN: 9780 86196 989 0
EPDF: ISBN: 9780 86196 990 6

Published by
John Libbey Publishing Ltd, 205 Crescent Road, East Barnet, Herts EN4 8SB,
United Kingdom
e-mail: libbeyj@truemail.co.th; web site: www.johnlibbey.com

Distributed worldwide by **Indiana University Press**,
Herman B Wells Library – 350, 1320 E. 10th St., Bloomington, IN 47405, USA.
www.iupress.indiana.edu

Printed and bound in Great Britain by Short Run Press Ltd, Exeter.

Table of Contents

Preface

Amanda Catto

It is a great honour to introduce this significant collection of essays exploring the work of Richard Demarco, the great artist, educator and champion of European culture and the Avant-garde in Scotland. Much has been written about Demarco, his pioneering activities and indomitable spirit but, surprisingly, there has been limited research into the Italo-Scottish collaborations and exchanges he has nurtured and sustained throughout his life. This publication adds considerable value to the existing canon of knowledge by providing fresh understandings of the impacts and influence of these relationships on the artists, institutions and collaborators involved. It also provides an excellent insight into the importance of Demarco's Italian heritage and the ways in which the country and culture of his ancestors has fundamentally shaped and informed his work and approach to life.

While focussed on the Italo-Scottish connection these essays do not attempt to define Demarco as a proponent of Italian art or as a promoter of Scottish art. Instead, they foreground Demarco's deep belief in artists and his lifelong commitment to enabling their ideas and ambitions through the spirit of collaboration and a unique ability to create points of connection.

As Demarco himself has said – 'There is no Polish art, or Scottish art, or English art, or Italian art. There is only art. And the great culture that binds us together as Europeans is also the culture of the world'.

Driven by a vision of art that is unfettered by nationalist ideals and a world set free of man-made borders, Demarco has travelled tirelessly in search of common histories and shared realities. Journeys encompassing art, philosophy and friendship can be seen as his 'modus operandi'. The act of travelling, mainly in the company of others, has been more important to Demarco than any final arrival or destination point. The Road to Meikle Seggie is both real and metaphorical, taking surprising turns and creating opportunities for profound spiritual and intellectual growth. In many respects, Demarco's journey is never ending. It is his personal quest for a better world, one where people can live together creatively, peacefully and at one with nature.

As a child Demarco experienced first-hand the tragic consequences of war, becoming acutely aware of the ways in which people are set against each other by forces outside of their control. Viciously bullied because of anti-Italian sentiment in Edinburgh during World War II he felt the pain of being judged to be something other, inferior, and out of place. This experience shaped him for life, making him an ardent and steadfast champion of people who find themselves on the outside, and the wrong side of societal norms. Demarco has an instinctive distrust of people whose power and authority can be easily abused and understands too well the impact this has on people's lives. Compelled to embrace alternative perspectives and to nurture new thinking, he revels in the opportunity to push boundaries and to defy those who would seek to curb or restrict his freedoms or the actions of others.

This publication confirms the status of Demarco as an Italo-Scot while emphasising his significance as an International-Scot. At a time of rapid globalisation, 24 hour news channels, cheap air travel and high speed digital connection it is impossible to fully appreciate Demarco's achievements in internationalising the arts in Scotland. That kind of work at that time took great energy, commitment, stamina and self-belief. Often the scope of his vision and ambition would butt up against the realities of logistics and resources and many projects were adapted or lost along the way. Remarkably, Demarco never allowed setbacks to diminish his vision, understanding that it is only by dreaming the impossible that the dream itself becomes possible.

Post-Brexit this publication creates the opportunity to both acknowledge and applaud Demarco's total commitment to Europe, as a cultural rather than a political or economic construct, a place where the realities of his ancestry and lineage are undeniable. In 2013 he was the first resident of the UK to be awarded the European Citizens' Prize in recognition of his efforts to strengthen European integration, cooperation and mutual understanding. As an Italian in Scotland he has always possessed an exceptional and innate openness to Europe, the avantgarde and the many different forms, styles and creative concerns it represents. Rejecting artworld trends he persisted in seeing value and potential in the work of European artists who had been overlooked or actively suppressed,

giving their work and ideas sufficient oxygen to breathe, develop and thrive.

It has been said that networks are Demarco's artworks and there are few people that possess such extensive and expansive connections within the world of the arts and society at large, both at home and abroad. His boundless energy and enthusiasm is infectious and like a modern-day pied piper he has been a consummate gatherer of people, adept at making introductions, starting conversations and letting ideas flow. A man of singular character Demarco is by no means a loner. A serial, and avid collaborator he has formed many friendships and experienced many fallouts, with each and every exchange leaving its mark.

Talking about his archive, Demarco often refers to it as being the collective endeavour of every artist that he has ever encountered, in recognition of the importance of the dialogue and discourse that has fuelled him from an early age. This publication is testament to the richness and diversity of material that the archive holds. It highlights the potential of this unique resource to act as the bedrock for future research and the catalyst for new knowledge building and exchange. Demarco's long held ambition is for the archive, in all its constituent parts, to be united under one roof and made accessible as a living and active resource that will spark and kindle new, creative collaborations and conversations. So many stories have been shared about Demarco and his achievements but, as these essays demonstrate, there is still much scope for new research and fresh enquiry.

Shaped in equal measure by his Italian ancestry and his life-long commitment to Scotland Demarco has made a unique and enriching contribution to the creative and cultural life of both countries. The legacies of his work run deep and in attending to these legacies new paths can be formed, new journeys planned and new forms of cultural and creative co-operation imagined.

I'd like to congratulate everybody involved in this publication for their remarkable essays and expert insights. I sincerely hope the sharing of these stories and histories will seed further interest and research into the life and work of a Richard Demarco – Italo-Scot, citizen of Europe and a truly remarkable man.

Amanda Catto is Head of Visual Arts, Creative Scotland

Introduction

Laura Leuzzi

Working variously as artist, gallery director, educator and cultural entrepreneur, Richard Demarco has cut a highly complex figure in the art world, having done so much to promote the European avant-garde in Scotland and internationally since the 1960s. Born an Italo-Scot, Demarco has devoted much of his time and efforts to promoting Italian art in Scotland and Scottish art in Italy.

Although his activities and legacy have been for a long time the subject of research and publications that have highlighted his endeavours,[1] little is known today about the cultural exchanges and relationships he initiated, developed and fostered between the two countries.

This gap in the historical canon of knowledge is extraordinary because in the Demarco archives – a portion of which is held by the Scottish National Gallery of Modern Art (SNGMA, (representing activities from 1963 to 1995) and a portion at the Demarco European Foundation (housed at the Summerhall in Edinburgh) – are many traces of exchanges between Italy and Scotland promoted by Demarco as part of his wider European network and contribution to the Edinburgh Festival. These documents – which have been partially digitised[2] – include photographs, ephemera, notes, catalogues and artworks that feature events involving important Italian or Italian-based artists, producers, performers, directors, critics including: Palma Bucarelli, the Count Panza di Biumo, Giulio Paolini, Jannis Kounellis, Bruno Ceccobelli, Toti Scialoja, Carlo Quartucci and Carla Tatò, Mimmo Rotella, Mario Merz, Fabrizio Plessi, Achille Bonito Oliva, Maria Gloria Conti Bicocchi, Giuseppe Chiari, Guido Sartorelli.

In 2018, Professors Elaine Shemilt and Stephen Partridge and I, with the support of Media Archivist Adam Lockhart, received funding from the Arts and Humanities Research Council to develop a research project at Duncan of Jordanstone College of Art and Design (University of Dundee) that would identify and reassess the most important of Demarco's Italo-Scottish exchanges, discussions, and relationships thus far marginalised in previous projects and publications.

Ultimately, this book is the main outcome of our research and retraces, uncovers and reassesses the cultural bridge between Scotland and Italy built by Demarco in a spirit of European co-operation and collaboration that has had a major impact and legacy in the UK both before and after Brexit.

The book consists of seven chapters and an appendix which together explore various different collaborations, connections and relationships, the aim being to foster and stimulate further research into Demarco's achievement and legacy. The first chapter, by Terri Colpi, lays the foundation for the entire book. In it Colpi, an internationally acclaimed expert on the

Figure 1: Richard Demarco and Giuliano Gori hugging the ash tree that was planted in La Fattoria di Celle to celebrate seven birthdays of his great friends – including Richard – in the Millennium Year of 2000, Fattoria di Celle, 2005.

Francesca Gallo in her chapter retraces in detail and with an international approach the germinal touring exhibition *Roma Punto Uno* organised by the famous Roman gallerist Mara Coccia. This touring exhibition underwent an important iteration at the Demarco Gallery, Edinburgh, in 1989.

Media Archivist Adam Lockhart in his chapter *The Celtic Connection* takes us on a journey through selected documents and ephemera from the Demarco archive using the powerful metaphor of the famous 'Road to Meikle Seggie'.

In his chapter, Marco Maria Gazzano discusses the germinal experimentation of La Zattera di Babele, complemented by an interview between Marina Bistolfi – organiser of their international events – and actress Carla Tatò – which uncovers how both the collaboration with Richard Demarco and the performance on Incholm Island in Scotland came about.

The 'Balkanist' Jonathan Blackwood focuses on Richard Demarco's celebrated relationships and exchanges with artists from the former Yugoslavia and how these interlaced with, and paralleled his Italian connections.

history of Italian migration, explores Demarco's family history and roots, discussing in depth the importance of his Italian heritage and situating his story in the wider context of the Italian diaspora.

My chapter unpacks and discusses the importance of the Italian connections for Demarco's activities in the late 1960s and the 1970s, from the early days of the Richard Demarco Gallery onwards. I pay particular attention to the exhibition *Contemporary Italian Art* (1967) and to the exchanges with the Galleria del Cavallino in Venice in the late 60s/early 70s.

Shemilt and Partridge for their part, interviewed Richard Demarco, their aim being to gather materials relating to, and to discuss the importance of his Italian heritage from his own perspective, between memories, historical traces and the present day.

In the appendix, a piece by Gabriella Cardazzo, once co-director of the internationally renowned Cavallino Gallery in Venice with her brother Paolo, gives the measure of the impact of Richard Demarco's activities upon artists, gallerists and performers alike, as well as the crucial importance of the human connections that were established in those years.

The appendix ends with a contribution by curator Deirdre Mackenna describing her curatorial approach to her programme *Richard Demarco. La strada, the route, the journey* at Castello Pandone in Molise, Italy.

I would like to take the opportunity in this introduction to thank on behalf of our research team all of the authors of the individual chapters and all the artists, critics, curators, and organisations who have contributed so generously to this project.

Last, but of course not least, our gratitude goes to Richard Demarco himself who supported, helped, stimulated and challenged us in our research, and ultimately inspired us, in a unique way to experience the European spirit that he has so truthfully promoted and continues to promote through the arts up until the present day.

Endnotes

1. These include for example the exhibition at the Royal Scottish Academy of Art and Architecture (27 November 2010 – 9 January 2011) and the book by E. McArthur & A. Watson (eds.), *10 Dialogues. Richard Demarco, Scotland and the European Avant Garde* (Edinburgh: Royal Scottish Academy of Art and Architecture, 2010).
2. The material became available online with the Demarco Digital Archive through a project based at University of Dundee by Watson/MacArthur/Shemilt initially funded by the AHRB/AHRC (2002–2008), with a Resource Enhancement Award 'The Demarco Archives: Accessing a 40-Year Dialogue between Richard Demarco and the European Avant-Garde'. 'The Demarco Archives' Project has been later developed into several follow-up projects, collaborations and events that saw the involvement of the CI (Shemilt) and the Archivist (Lockhart). *Richard Demarco: The Italian Connection* would capitalise on these projects, and the participation of the CI and Archivist would be a key facilitating factor.

Acknowledgements

Richard Demarco | The Italian Connection is the main output of the eponymous research project funded by the Arts and Humanities Research Council and based at Duncan of Jordanstone College of Art and Design, University of Dundee. The research team consisted of Dr Laura Leuzzi, Professor Stephen Partridge, and Adam Lockhart, led by Professor Elaine Shemilt.

A special thank you goes to Richard Demarco and the Demarco European Foundation for their inspiring guidance in this journey.

We wish to thank all the authors, artists, performers, copyeditors, translators and our publisher without whose dedication and passion, this volume could not have been achieved.

This book would have not been possible without the generous contribution of all the artists, curators, academics, theoreticians, practitioners, technicians, galleries, museums, libraries and archives that have participated in the project. To each and all of them we owe our immense gratitude. Hopefully this publication justifies their trust in us.

Special thanks go to the Italian Cultural Institute in Edinburgh for their constant support.

Courtesy of all images – if not otherwise specified – is of the Demarco Digital Archive, University of Dundee and The Demarco Archive.

1

Navigating Italian Migration to Scotland: Richard Demarco and the Ricardian Road

Terri Colpi

Introduction

Many aspects of the historic Italian migration to Scotland have been researched,[1] but any consideration of how *Cavaliere* Richard Demarco[2] fits into this movement of people and its chronicle and, more so, how he as an individual has been shaped by his Italian heritage, has never previously been critically evaluated. Cursory mention is often given to Demarco being 'Italo-Scot',[3] which is usually then linked to his acclaimed Europeanness. Yet, detail or understanding of his Italian ancestry has been ignored or, more usually, reliant on misinformation and mythology. Perhaps seemingly peripheral to the study of Demarco's monumental contribution to the arts, this chapter by contrast places not only his forebears but also the history and milieu of the Italian community at its heart and seeks to spotlight the influence of this uncharted but important landscape.

Born in 1930 in Edinburgh and christened Ricardo, three of Demarco's grandparents were Italian, the fourth being Irish Italian. As fourth generation Italian on one side of the family and between third and fourth on the other, a socio-temporal situation often associated with some distance from immigrant tradition, Demarco can nevertheless be understood as influenced by the history and culture of this minority group. The chapter begins by documenting family migration, exploring artistic inheritance, moves through discussions of kinship, community and Catholicity, examines Demarco's escape from the 'ghetto' and his relationship with Italianness and Italy, finally considering the emergence of the 'Euro-Scot'. By unpicking family history from the accepted narrative, one that Demarco himself has helped construct, and by contextualising his experiences and their negotiation within the historic Italian migration to Scotland, the aim here is to offer new insight into Demarco's origin, journey and European destination.

Migration Portraits

The migration of Demarco's ancestors illustrates archetypal portraits of Scotland's historic Italian families, particularly those originally from the culturally distinctive Ciociaria.[4] This essentially rural, mountainous territory between Rome and Naples became a major source of emigration after Italian Unification in 1861 and the hardships and upheavals wrought on the agrarian economy. Fanning out across Europe, largely on foot, the migrants were itinerant and, despite their illiteracy, creative and adaptable. 'Chains of migration' formed and followed paths through France, often with sojourns in Paris, to London and then elsewhere in the UK. Intermittent periods at 'home' were common and final family relocation could take many years. In subsequent generations, transnational links to origin villages were typically maintained. Street entertainment playing unique, homemade instruments such as *zampogne*, a type of bagpipe,[5] and later, street vending of rudimentary foods, were characteristic early means of support.

Particularly interesting here, however, was another thread within this migration: a distinct segment who became famous across Europe as artists' models. Deriving from an earlier tradition of modelling in Rome for 'grand tour' artists wearing distinctive Ciociaria costume, the models, both male and female, were renowned for their perfect physiques, flawless skin and distinctive features and became much sought after in Paris and London. Michele Santulli has researched the identities of individual models and contends that the development of artistic modelling as a profession can be attributed to the Ciociari who, furthermore, being amongst the most widespread in western art, contributed to the transmission of the canon of classical Mediterranean beauty.[6] Santulli argues that these models were more influential in art history than has been appreciated; their creative and inspirational input to artistic works evinced their familiarity with western iconographical tradition and the ways of the atelier. Susan Waller similarly states that the models' performance on the stand expressed a collective artistic knowledge nurtured and refined within the expatriate Italian communities, giving them an instinctive understanding of representations of historical narratives.[7] From the 1870s, Santulli estimates over a thousand Ciociari models in Paris, the best employed by Cézanne, Matisse, Van Gogh, Picasso and Rodin and confirms that, although fewer in number, the models employed in London were mostly from the village of Picinisco. Unaware of their specific and shared geographical origin and tradition, Scott Thomas Buckle nonetheless names some Ciociari models active contemporaneously in London: Angelo Colarossi who modelled for Sargent, Leighton and Millais; Domenico Mancini for Holman Hunt, Watts, Draper and Sargent; Antonia Caira for Blake Richmond and Burne-Jones; Gaetano Meo for Rossetti and Burne-Jones.[8] Mancini's son, Vincenzo and Colarossi's son, also called Angelo, posed respectively for George Frampton's Peter Pan sculpture in Kensington Gardens and Eros by Albert Gilbert at Piccadilly Circus.[9] One model, Alessandro De Marco, possibly a distant relative of Demarco, arrived in London in 1867.[10] Considered to be 'the living embodiment of classical beauty', he posed for Millais, Poynter, Legros and Burne-Jones,[11] while his son Antonio also modelled at the Royal Academy.[12]

As a child, Demarco unwittingly participated in this modelling tradition when he posed for a portrait, Edinburgh artist Betty Maxton having recognised in him the 'face of a Mantegna angel'.[13] Not only a retrospectively symbolically significant echo of Demarco's cultural heritage, this is conceivably the first tangible connection to his future world; Maxton also introduced Demarco to the Scottish National Gallery. Around this very time, apparently unknown to Demarco, the pre-Raphaelite model Domenico Mancini, was living close to the Demarco family in Portobello, Edinburgh. In 1928, at the age of fifty-five, Mancini had relocated from London and throughout the 1930s he worked 'in winter' as an artists' model in Edinburgh.[14] Later, however, in the 1950s, as a student at Edinburgh College of Art, one of the last artists to draw Domenico Mancini, by then some eighty years old and considered 'the last Italian model' of the iconographic tradition of migrants from Picinisco, was Richard Demarco (see Figure 1).

De Marco Family – Italian and French Influences

The narrative of Demarco's Italian heritage usually begins with his father, previous generations remaining unaccounted. Yet, a further two generations back we find a direct link to the modelling tradition discussed above.[15] Demarco's paternal great-grandfather, Carmino De Marco,[16] born in 1822 in Picinisco, was an artists' model, most probably in Paris, giving clear family connection to this unique legacy and engendering familiarity with Paris. Although five of Carmino's six children, including Demarco's paternal grandfather, Antonio, were born in Picinisco between 1845 and 1859, one son was born in Paris in 1856. It is not inconceivable that family members were present during Carmino's modelling sojourns, even themselves working as models. Jill Berk Jiminez states that 'Posing was a family business among Italians, and men, women, and children, the very young and the very old, posed individually or in groups for painters, sculptors and photographers'.[17] Certainly, three of Carmino's sons lived in Paris as

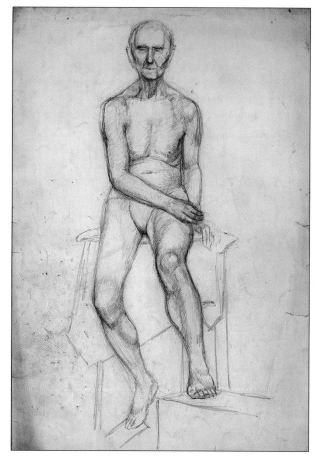

Figure 1: Drawing of Domenico Mancini at Edinburgh College of Art by Richard Demarco. [Copyright The Demarco Archive.]

young adults – notably for Demarco's story – Michele whose own son Gabriele was Parisian-born in 1877 and Antonio (Demarco's grandfather) whose eldest child Maria Cristina was born in Paris c.1880.

As other family members and younger generations identified new opportunities, family migration trajectories adjusted. Glasgow became such a destination for the extended De Marco family in the late 1880s; by 1895 Antonio and several of his brothers were located there.[18] Carmino himself died in Glasgow in 1899, aged 77, at 409 Parliamentary Road. Recorded on a son's wedding certificate in 1903 as 'artists modeller' (deceased), and indicating his last occupation, it is not inconceivable that Carmino found employment at Glasgow

School of Art at a time when its director, Francis Henry Newberry, was 'in the habit of employing male Italians for life classes'.[19] Five of Carmino's six sons successively moved with their families to the east coast, especially around Edinburgh. When Demarco's father, named Carmino after his grandfather, was born at Dunbar in 1901,[20] Antonio was already established in Musselburgh with an ice-cream business. Although both paternal grandparents were deceased when Demarco was born in 1930,[21] the network of descendants from their generation who had inter-married with other Frosinone families present in Scotland – Arcari, Capaldi, Corio, Crolla, D'Ambrosio, De Luzio, Pelosi – was extensive (see Figure 2). The scale of Demarco numbers alone is evidenced by three sets of first cousin marriages in Demarco's father's generation.

It is through Antonio and his elder brother Michele, and their children, Maria Cristina and Gabriele born and raised in Paris, that we trace the origins of the Demarco empire in Portobello, at its

height in the 1930s as young Ricardo, 'Rico', was growing up. Cousins Maria Cristina and Gabriele married in 1901, consolidating their controlling position in the family business. Twenty-two years older than her sibling Carmino, Maria Cristina became the driving force, by 1925 personally owning much of the promenade. Beyond the increasingly successful 'Maison Demarco', her property included several flats and shops, often let to other Italians, fair ground, kiosks, lock-ups, dressing rooms and stage and prop stores.[22] Named *Maison Demarco* to reflect the family's time in Paris, and seemingly fashioned on the French café, Demarco underscores the French influence. In romantic embellishment he even suggests that the family surname had been 'frenchified' from Di Marco to De Marco,[23] belying De Marco ancestors who can be traced back to the 1700s in Picinisco.[24] The business model of Maison Demarco with its fusion of French, Italian and contemporary British art nouveau influences, its finery and high quality of service, was 'state of the

Figure 2: Demarco-Arcari Wedding, 1915. Gabriele and Maria Cristina Demarco, back row, 2nd and 3rd on right. Carmino Demarco, sitting on floor, 1st on left. [Copyright Terri Colpi Archive Collection.]

Figure 3: Coffee Cup and Silver Plated Milk Jug from Maison Demarco.

Figure 4: Drawing of Maison Demarco interior by Richard Demarco, 1947.
[Copyright The Demarco Archive.]

art' (see Figure 3). Comparable Italian family businesses were not uncommon, however, in this era, especially at the popular coastal resorts. In the Franchitti family's *Café de Paris* in Motherwell, we detect similar French connections. The Demarco ice-cream business continued in tandem at Portobello run by Antonio and his other children, including Carmino. Demarco has described his father making ice-cream,[25] but this activity with lowlier and specifically Italian immigrant connotations resonates less ap-

pealingly or as culturally significant with him compared to the glamour of the *Maison* (see Figure 4). Carmino also worked as a manager at Maison Demarco but, in 1949 when Maria Cristina died, it was Umberto her son who inherited, transforming the business into an 'American Soda Parlour' in the 1950s.[26]

In the received narrative of Demarco's life, the cultural legacy of Maison Demarco is emphasised as inspirational not only for Demarco's own self-conception but also for the organisation of his art galleries some thirty years later. In an autobiographical essay Demarco sets out the terrain

> Maison Demarco was the very model I had in the back of my mind when I first dreamt of The Traverse Theatre and The Demarco Gallery, as places where all the arts could be enjoyed in a convivial atmosphere of good food and drink with more than a touch of the Continental way of life.[27]

He describes the elegant ambience of Maison Demarco, highlighting French and European aspects, making no mention of the Italian

> ... the Demarco family ... built this most beautiful manifestation of life in Paris. Everything was Parisian. The wood came from Paris. The tabletops where you got your coffee were marble, the stained-glass windows were art nouveau. ...There was certainly music. ... It was the world of the *thé dansant*. ... Maison Demarco was the name given to a way of life. ... It was completely European...[28]

Demarco's wish to expand the European imagery can be perceived in Giles Sutherland's assertion '*Maison Demarco was modelled on the idea of a European café, of the kind found in Kraków or Paris*'.[29] The unusual reference to Kraków suggests co-authorship by Demarco, reweaving the family story to include allusion to his work in Poland, again omitting Italy. Despite relegation in the narrative, we must nevertheless presume the Italian ingredient, French and Italian cultures collaging to articulate Europeanness to a Scottish clientele. Demarco has described his father as 'intensely Italian',[30] typecasting Carmino as the consummate '*bella figura*' and providing example for Demarco to position himself *as a* European cultural host

> He was a remarkable man, much loved by everybody who met him, charming, urbane, handsome, dapper, well-

dressed. ... He was a man of great charm, elegance and the perfect *maître d'*... that's what I am. I am the person who welcomes people into a world that is one-hundred-percent European.[31]

There is no doubt the pre-war reality of Maison Demarco left an indelible impression on Demarco, its transcultural topography eventually forming a mythologised European underpinning. However, his reframing disregards the commercial drive of the 1930s establishment to generate profit, Demarco stressing he never envisioned or operated his galleries as moneymaking enterprises or 'art shops'. His transposition from the ingrained bedrock of economic self-sufficiency and financial success upon which the Italian community was founded, and indeed remained rooted in the 1960s, to a variously 'funded' environment, was in itself a significant break with tradition and departure from expectation.

Fusco Family – Irish and Catholic Influences

Turning to Demarco's mother's family, equally interesting and again not atypical migration portraits are evident. Maternal great-grandfather, Luigi Fusco was born 1840 in Villa Latina,[32] a few miles from Picinisco, and was among the early Ciociari arrivals in the British Isles after Italian Unification. Described as 'a wonderful adventurer', family oral history recounts that Luigi had fought as a lieutenant in the Papal army against Garibaldi, about which Demarco, disapproving of Unification, is immensely proud.[33] By 1870, mostly on foot and likely in the company of compatriots, Luigi had journeyed up through France, crossed the English Channel and also the Irish Sea. In Ireland, he met Dublin-born widow Elizabeth Chiaverini (neé

McGuinness);[34] in 1875 Demarco's maternal grandfather, Giovanni – 'John' – Fusco, was born in Belfast.[35] Although the enclave from Frosinone was growing in Belfast, by 1891 Luigi and Elizabeth had gravitated to Edinburgh's larger Italian colony where Luigi had relatives and Elizabeth was joined by two of three daughters from her first marriage. Their accommodation at 291 Cowgate with a shop attached to living quarters had been tenanted by the Fusco family since 1880.

In 1898 John Fusco married Maria Brattesani, also a second generation Italian, born in Leith in 1878. Similar to the Demarco family, the previous Brattesani generation had sojourned in France during their northward progression, Maria's elder sister Valentina being Parisian-born. Unusually for Scotland's Italians, however, the Brattesani family originated in Borgotaro,[36] Parma, in northern Italy and represented a much less numerous contingent than migrants from Frosinone or, the other main source, the Lucca area of Tuscany.[37] This early 'mixed' marriage of Maria and John, of northern and southern Italian origin, was uncommon, the two culturally distinct groups generally making endogamous spouse choices as late at the 1930s.[38] Perhaps even more significant than the contrasting Italian roots, however, was the Irish connection. Leaving Edinburgh and returning to the land of his birth and his mother's native soil, John had a brief period back in Ireland with Maria where Demarco's mother, Elizabeth Fusco, was born in County Down in 1901.[39]

It is credible that John Fusco identified strongly with Ireland, considering himself equally Irish and Italian. His marriage into the Brattesani family would have reinforced his sense of *italianità*, but as Demarco recognises, his 'Fusco family was not quite Italian' and comprised

'a mix of two types of Italians'.[40] Despite John's father Luigi, at 70, living with the couple in 1911, by then owning a flat and shop in Portobello, it is improbable they spoke 'Italian' as a family.[41] With John and Maria being British-born and their parents' village dialects from Villa Latina and Borgotaro mutually incomprehensible, familial communication in English seems more practicable. From their eleven children, by now the third generation, only three chose Italian spouses, including Elizabeth who married Carmino Demarco in 1928. (See Figure 5). One son was ordained a priest in Rome; an unmarried daughter became a housekeeper to Catholic priests while the other six married within the Catholic Church, mostly to spouses of Irish descent. It was the deeply Catholic nature of the Fusco family,[42] together with Catholic schooling,[43] that affected and cultivated Demarco's love of the beauty, liturgy and 'theatre' of the Mass and sacramental life. The associated cultural manifestations of art – Michelangelo's *Pietà* first revealed in a 'holy picture' given to Demarco by his Brattesani grandmother – music and Latin within the Church added to his religious appreciation. However, it was Demarco's first visit to Italy, to Rome, in 1950, during Holy Year that brought epiphany of the univer-

Figure 5: Demarco's parents, Elizabeth Valentina Fusco and Carmino Demarco. [Courtesy Helen Quilietti Stanton.]

sality and centrality of Catholicism, providing integrated scaffolding to key determinants – Italianness, Catholicity and Europeanness.

As Demarco's philosophy and interest in the history of ideas evolved, the high culture of Catholicism perhaps more than any other factor shaped his worldview. Encompassing such concepts as being, truth, beauty, love and art, it became central. Demarco's personal lexicon articulates 'Catholic' words and spiritual concepts – souls, communion of saints, sacred sites, pilgrimages. Many of these, for example, the 'sacred nature of time' would bear deep theological and philosophical discourse. Contention that 'all good art ascends to the condition of prayer',[44] and his unique interdisciplinary approach towards all mankind's interactions with our planet are reinforced by personal transcultural links with Benedictine monks, catholic academics and thinkers across Europe. For Demarco, that Saint Benedict, patron saint of Europe, established his monastery at Monte Cassino is a more powerful tie to his native area of Italy than the

presence today of De Marco or Fusco relatives in Picinisco or Villa Latina, with whom he has no meaningful relationship.[45]

Family and Community

By the 1930s, the Italians in Scotland had achieved stability, the majority of families owning small businesses trading in ice-cream and confectionery or foods, particularly fish and chips. A 1933 Italian census evidences that virtually all male respondents were self-employed, the nuclear family forming the economic backbone of the community.[46] The Fusco family's Marine Café, also on the promenade at Portobello, was a classic endeavour. By contrast, Maison Demarco epitomised a pinnacle of success and was capable of supporting the extended family. In 1930, Carmino, aged thirty, was enabled to branch out to launch the *Trocadéro* on Edinburgh's Princess Street facsimiled on Maison Demarco, but which failed within a year. According to Demarco, his father's spirit was broken by this fiasco, although

Figure 6: The Demarco Family, c.1938. 'Rico' stands beside his father. [Copyright The Demarco Archive.]

ELIZABETH VALENTIA DEMARCO   LOUIS DEMARCO   MICHAEL DEMARCO   RICO DEMARCO   CARMINO (CAR) DEMARCO

sented the very essence of the transcultural European spirit that Demarco sought to promote and uphold and, forming a bridge or space between two worlds, Maison Demarco became routinely employed as the conduit for comment on family heritage and even self.

Meanwhile, fellow Italian Scots were similarly emerging to redefine the cultural landscape and rising to prominence in the arts, especially visual. Informatively, Eduardo Paolozzi, Jack Vettriano [Vettraino], Alberto Morrocco [Marrocco] and Antonio Pacitti, like Demarco, all had origins in the Ciociaria, leading back to the familiarity with art outlined earlier.[87] While Demarco sensed Vettriano's comparable reaction to Scotland – a longing to be part of something bigger – and through his paintings the creation of a different, exotic milieu,[88] there was little engagement amongst this group. Caricaturist Emilio Coia,[89] (see Figure 8) however, intersected with Demarco's world, not only sketching portraits of Demarco but also being invited to draw avant-garde theatre director Tadeusz Kantor in 1973.[90] In the 1980s, dialogue with Lord Charles Forte, arguably the most successful Ciociaria migrant of his generation, encouraged Demarco to reconsider their common heritage: the artists' models in Forte's collection of nineteenth century oil paintings; the importance of the farmer as architect and curator of the rural landscape; the concept of their being 'children of Cicero', the great Roman polymath from Arpino in the Ciociaria.[91] It is this last, abstract and timeless 'idea' of Italy and its esteemed inheritance with which Demarco most identifies – 'I come from a world where classical Greco-Romano culture is spectacularly revealed and defended'.[92] He espouses and interacts intellectually with an unbound space-time continuum from classical civilisation and renais-

Figure 8: Emilio Coia and Richard Demarco. Outside The Demarco Gallery, 8 Melville Crescent, Edinburgh, 1967. [Copyright The Demarco Archive.]

sance genius to contemporary art of today.

In Edinburgh, Demarco's 'outsider' and non-establishment footing stimulated and cultivated his originality. Similar to Paolozzi who was 'enduringly unsure of his own place in the landscape',[93] Demarco's occupancy of in-between spaces and affinity with being 'other' gave him an edge that proved inimitable in stretching his natural creativity towards innovative and often challenging ideas. Timothy Neat goes further, describing Demarco as an 'apolitical radical' who instinctively questions authority and rebels against accepted ways of doing things,[94] earning him the appellation 'maverick'. Nevertheless, it was the energies and internationalism of the Festival that nurtured a symbiotic relationship and secured Demarco's lasting commitment to Edinburgh. Significantly, Demarco turned in 1967 to Italy for his first international exhibition at the Demarco Gallery, presenting 'Contemporary Italian Art'. His 1968 visit to the Venice Biennale can be seen as seminal in his dialogue with Italy, Italian artists and galleries from which important collaborations emerged, evolved and have been sustained. The visionary collectors Count Panza di Biumo and Giuliano Gori and the Galleria del Cavallino are names that spring to mind along with some of

Figure 9: Caffè Florian, Venice by Richard Demarco, 2000. [Courtesy Demarco Archive.]

the many Italian artists Demarco brought to Edinburgh such as Anselmo Anselmi, Paolo Patelli and Giancarlo Venuto. Demarco's relationship with Venice and its months long bi-annual arts extravaganza, perhaps more than any other Italian city, has provided inspiration and synergy through which the Edinburgh Festival has undoubtedly been nourished. In 2000, Demarco literally brought Venice to Edinburgh with his suite of Venetian watercolours exhibited at the Howard Hotel (see Figure 9) where a physical recreation of piazza San

Marco's famous Caffè Florian was also staged. This dynamic was reversed in its climactic exhibition of 2019 when, at the historic Scuola Grande di San Marco in Venice, Demarco presented The Demarco Archive through his 'Art and Healing' retrospective, paying tribute to all those who have accompanied him on his journey.[95]

Demarco developed contacts and collaborations across other fields as his interdisciplinarity and ability to see beyond boundaries blossomed; his *Pentagonale Plus* events of the early 1990s at Kingston University and in Edinburgh with Gianni De Michelis, Italy's Foreign Minister, a spectacular example of bringing the world of European politics into focus through the lens of the arts. In this regard, Demarco's role as a cultural mediator creating links between Scotland and Italy is unsurpassed and both countries owe him a huge debt. However, this relationship was far from exclusive as Demarco's dialogues became increasingly trans European, crossing aesthetic and geopolitical borders, especially encompassing eastern European countries before the end of the Cold War. Establishment of the Demarco European Art Foundation in 1992 and appointment as Professor of European Cultural Studies at Kingston University 1993 consolidated the cultural patrimony and 'Europeanness' that he now fully embodied. Albeit foundational, Italo-Scottish heritage had become subsidiary as European identity and recognition crystallised; the 'Euro-Scot' had fully metamorphosed. In 2013, the European Commission acknowledged Demarco's work by awarding him the European Citizens' Medal, the first UK resident to be so honoured.

Recontouring the Road

The Italian community in Scotland has evolved and changed immeasurably in the last twenty or thirty years as indeed has Scottish society itself with its more tolerant and inclusive dimensions in addition to its European affinities. Descendants of the historic migration, now between fourth and sixth generations, typically consider themselves only partly Italian and represent diversity in many spheres of activity. Nevertheless a hyphenated or hybrid cultural identity persists, which today is recognised and valued, especially when set within the commodification of things Italian and Ital-

ian Scots' contribution to the arts generally.[96] From around 2000, the 'community' also encompasses and has been enriched by the substantial wave of 'new' Italian migrants, from all over Italy, operating across many professional, academic and artistic fields. It could be argued that Demarco has reoriented somewhat towards the now more varied and vibrant presence of *italianità,* finding more commonality. He has encouraged those presenting works on Italian Scottish culture, for example, staging Margaret Rose's *Scars of War* play at the Demarco-Rocket venue in 2002, assisting Laura Pasetti develop the script for *A Bench on the Road*, 2014, performed around Scotland and at the Piccolo Teatro, Milan and embracing Deirdre McKenna's Cultural Documents in 2019, acknowledging their shared origin. (See Appendix Two). By presenting an exhibition of his own work depicting the iconic Italian source villages of the historic migrants to Scotland at Valvona & Crolla food emporium in Edinburgh in 2005, Demarco demonstrably linked himself to Italian Scottish heritage. As new cultural entrepreneurs have emerged, such as Professor Federica Pedriali of Edinburgh University, initiating dialogues between Scotland, Italy and the Italian community, Demarco has participated – notably in 2013 at a diaspora conference at Cassino University and the Gadda prize held at Monte Cassino Abbey.[97] Professional filmmaker, Marco Federici is the first family member to enter Demarco's orbit,[98] sitting on The Demarco Archive's board from 2018, entrusted with documenting events and retrospectively building the cinematographic account of Demarco's life's work (see Figure 10).[99] As interest in 'Italian Scotland' has stimulated a growing literature in autobiography, fiction, drama and academic publication, support from the European Commis-

sion's Cultural Programme, 'Seeing Stories' and the Italian Cultural Institute, rendered Demarco's 1978 monograph to be republished with Italian translation in 2015.[100]

It also seems that in old age Demarco often turns pensively to the world of his forefathers through works such as the book 'Pastorizia' by the late Luigi Giannetti on sheep farming in Abruzzo with its photographs of the prehistoric rock carvings and paintings made by shepherds in the caves above Picinisco.[101] With this frame of mind, recovery of intrinsic Italianness and becoming 'Rico' again is perceptible, yet, at the same time, Demarco continues to transfer and translate his endeavour forward in many meaningful conversations with Italy today.[102] However, while beyond the scope of this chapter, it must be reiterated that Demarco's association with Italy is not exclusionary since with profound sentience for the human condition he continues to respond through the transcultural language of art to human creativity all across Europe. That said, it must be acknowledged that, ultimately, his relationship with Italy is unique since it is the Italian peninsula that Demarco regards as the land where mankind has consistently reached its peak creativity and civilisation; in this sense, it is in his Italian connection that he truly recognises his inheritance.

Conclusion

This chapter has explored and deconstructed certain prevailing mythologies that have thus far clouded Demarco's family history. The contextual optic of the historic Italian migration to Scotland has facilitated further insight to the man's life and times and some new perspective on Demarco's relationship with Italy has been revealed. There is little doubt the colossus that is Richard Demarco, with his unparalleled contribution in the last seventy years to dialogue between Scotland and Europe, is matchless. Formation of this virtuosity must be set within two contexts. Firstly, his Italian heritage, from as he sees it, Cicero, Saint Benedict and the patina of family interludes in Paris, endowed him with a special affinity towards Europe. Secondly, growing up and permanently resident in Scotland, feeling cut-off from the cultural and spiritual heartland of Europe prescribed a yearning for this other world; to connect and interact with it became his defining life's goal. Moreover, his 'outsider' status in Edinburgh, with all the challenges this entailed, combined with an instinctive desire to educate both native Scots and others in the philosophical and artistic truths of Europe, ensured the on-going tension that stimulated his creativity and allowed him to act within a space outside the mainstream. Ultimately, the dynamism of the Edinburgh Festival provided the crucible and platform to sustain Demarco over a lifetime's work, fashioning his remarkable contribution not only to the history of the arts but also to the narrative of Italian presence in Scotland.

As a final thought, return to the example of the artists' models with whom we began seems apt, for Demarco's journey expresses a profoundly resonant echo of this ancestral *modus vivendi et operandi*. His deep pull towards the arts, instinct to take risks and to traverse and encompass Europe seem almost infused with genetic memory of the rhetoric of art, the atelier and the inter-connection of the creative processes. Following in the footsteps of the Ciociari who spread Mediterranean beauty and civilization through their contribution to art, Demarco's mission has fostered a new chapter in this dialogue and connection between Scotland and Italy. In this sense alone, in setting his course along the Ricardian road, always alert to and guided by the 'offing', that original in-between space, Demarco has navigated towards a pan-European artistic arena and a centuries old cultural exchange of people and ideas.

Endnotes

1. Lucio Sponza, *Italian Immigrants in Nineteenth Century Britain: Realities and Images* (Leicester: Leicester University Press, 1988), pp. 108–115; Nicoletta Franchi, *La Via della Scozia. L'emigrazione Barghigiana e Lucchese a Glasgow tra Ottocento e Novecento* (Lucca: Fondazione Paolo Cresci, 2012); Terri Colpi, *Italians' Count in Scotland. Recording History, The 1933 Census* (London: The St James Press, 2015).
2. Cavaliere Ordine al Merito della Repubblica Italiana, Knight of the Italian Republic, awarded 1987.
3. Demarco has long self-described as 'Italo-Scot'. 'Scottish' or 'Scots Italian' is used by the Italian community, while 'Italian Scot' is employed by academics conforming to the Italian diaspora literature (Italian Americans etc.).
4. The Ciociaria corresponds roughly to Frosinone province in the Lazio region.
5. For photograph of De Marco family group of musicians at Mons, Belgium c.1900, see Colpi, *Italians' Count*, p. 68.
6. Michele Santulli, *Modelle e Modelli Ciociari nell'Arte Europea, a Roma, Parigi, Londra nel 1800–1900* (Arpino: Edizione Ciociaria Sconosciuta, 2010).
7. Susan Waller, 'Rodin and the Modèle Italien', *Sculpture Journal*, 27.1 (2018), 75–88.
8. Scott Thomas Buckle, 'Is this the Face of Alessandro di Marco? The Forgotten Features of a Well-Known Italian Model', *The British Art Journal*, 13.2 (2012), 67–75.
9. Michele Santulli, 'Modelli Ciociari in Pubblico a Londra', 8 Jan 2019. Available online: https://www.inciociaria.org/2019/01/08/modelli-ciociari-in-pubblico-a-londra/ [accessed 10 June 2021]; Colin Ford, 'Angelo Colarossi – Two Artists' Models', *History of Photography*, 28.4 (2004), 180–181.
10. In English language references, sometimes misspelt as di Marco (see Endnote 8). Santulli identifies Alessandro as De Marco and Millais correctly records him as De Marco in six sittings at the Royal Academy in 1871. Antonia Caira is also misnamed as 'Caiva' by Buckle (p. 68) and 'Cura' by others.
11. Michele Santulli, 'Val Comino: L'Arte nei Secoli ha il Volto della Ciociaria', 10 Sept 2016. Available online: http://www.antonellocaporale.it/2016/09/10/alfabeto-michele-santulli-val-comino-larte-nei-secoli-ha-il-volto-della-ciociaria/ [accessed 15 June 2021].
12. Models' Receipts 1897-1902. Royal Academy of Arts, RRA/TRE/7/1.
13. Norah Carlin, *Holy Cross Academy, Edinburgh. The Life and Times of a Catholic School, 1907–1969* (Edinburgh: New Cut Press, 2009), p. 96.
14. Colpi, *Italians' Count*, p. 81.
15. Genealogical research based on: Birth, Marriage and Death records, National Records Scotland (NRS); Antenati, Italian State Archives; Census Returns 1881, 1891, 1901 and 1911 (NRS). I am grateful to Nello Ostacchini of the Anglo Italian Family History Society, Stuart Capaldi and Helen Quilietti Stanton for their generous help in tracing records. See www.capaldi-clan.com and www.quiliettifamily.com [accessed 13 March 2021].
16. De Marco was anglicised by officials, appearing in documentation as Demarco from 1881.
17. Jill Berk Jiminez, *Dictionary of Artists' Models* (Abingdon: Routledge, 2013), pp. 17–18.
18. Siblings of Carmino De Marco also migrated to Glasgow and to south coast resorts where descendants still live. Demarco's brother, Michael, moved to Bournemouth to join this branch of the family, where his sons live today.
19. Joseph Farrell, 'The Integration Game: How Italo-Scots shaped Scotland', *Barga News*, 29 Jun 2018. Available online: https://www.barganews.com/2018/06/29/the-integration-game-how-italo-scots-shaped-scotland/ [accessed 4 October 2021].
20. Not Kelty in Fife as normally specified and not Carmine, as sometimes stated. Carmine was, however, also a family name: Demarco's father Carmino had an uncle Carmine as well as a first cousin called Carmine.

21. Antonio Demarco died in 1927, his wife, Maria Giuseppina Corio, in 1915.

22. NRS, Valuation Rolls, 1905–1935.

23. Richard Demarco, *National Life Stories. Artists' Lives*, interviews by Jenny Simmons, Recordings 1-64 (British Library Sounds, 2005-2007), Recording 1. Available online: https://sounds.bl.uk/Arts-literature-and-performance/Art/021M-C0466X0242XX-0001V0 [accessed 25 January 2021]. Henceforth BLSA, R1-64. More recently, see also Mandy Rhodes, 'Holding Back the Years', *Holyrood Magazine*, 6 April 2020. Available online: https://www.holyrood.com/inside-politics/view,holding-back-the-years-interview-with-richard-demarco_15332.htm [accessed 20 July 2021].

24. Demarco's great-great-grandfather, Francesco De Marco, was born in Picinisco, 1785.

25. BLSA, R1.

26. No photographs of Maison Demarco could be traced. For 1959 image of American Soda Parlour, see https://www.scran.ac.uk/database/record.php?usi=000-000-066-262 [accessed 20 July 2021].

27. Richard Demarco, 'Too Rough To Go Slow', in Paul Henderson Scott, ed., *Spirits of the Age: Scottish Self-Portraits* (Edinburgh: Saltire Society, 2005), pp. 87–122 (p. 93).

28. Giles Sutherland, 'On the Road to Meikle Seggie. Richard Demarco's Edinburgh Arts Journeys 1972-80' (PhD Thesis, University of Dundee, 2020), p. 100.

29. Sutherland, p. 99.

30. BLSA, R1.

31. Sutherland, pp. 100–101.

32. Demarco names his maternal great-grandfather as Giovanni Fusco (Demarco 'Too Rough To Go Slow', p. 88; BLSA, R2 [accessed 29 January 2021]), but he is recorded as Luigi in Antenati, the 1911 Census and on son John Fusco's marriage certificate. The 1891 Census records him as Lewis, then commonly used for Luigi (see also Endnote 39).

33. BLSA, R2.

34. Elizabeth Maginness (or McGuinness), born c.1840, married Jacopo Pasquale Chiaverini (or Chiavarini, anglicised to Chaverini/Chavarini) an Italian immigrant in Dublin c.1857. The couple lived in Dublin and Cork, but by 1866 were settled in Belfast.

35. Jacopo Chiaverini died in 1877 and is recorded on John's birth certificate as his father. Both John and his younger brother Joseph, were adopted by Luigi Fusco when he married Elizabeth McGuinness Chiaverini.

36. For reasons unknown, and despite acknowledged second cousins of Brattesani descent living in Edinburgh today, Demarco has stated that his maternal grandmother had origins in Barga, Lucca (BLSA, R2; Demarco, 'Too Rough to Go Slow', p. 89). This misinformation has been reiterated by several authors, for example, Donald Smith, 'The Road Goes On', in Richard Demarco, *The Road to Meikle Seggie* (Edinburgh: Luath Press, 2015), pp. 11–21 (p. 11) and Laura Leuzzi, 'Edimburgo-Roma 1967. Connessioni italo-scozzesi sulle tracce della mostra Contemporary Italian Art alla Richard Demarco Gallery', *Storia dell'Arte*, 1/2 (2019), 205–215 (p. 206).

37. Colpi, *Italians' Count*, pp. 102–105. Migrants from Borgotaro settled primarily in London, with comparatively few families in Scotland, located mainly in Aberdeen and the northeast.

38. Colpi, *Italians' Count*, pp. 123–124.

39. John and Maria's first born child, named Luigi, indicating his grandfather's name, had been born in Edinburgh in 1899 and died there in 1903 after the family's return from Ireland.

40. BLSA, R2.

41. Standard Italian did not become widespread in Italy until after World War Two.

42. BLSA, R2. John Fusco was a lay Franciscan. Demarco family Catholicism was less devout (BLSA, R4, R5 [accessed 15 February 2021]).

43. Catholic churches and schools in Scotland were Hibernian in character. As a child, Demarco was aware of the differences between Italian and Irish Catholicism (BLSA, R5).

44. Demarco, 'Too Rough To Go Slow', p. 121. He asserts also that a Morandi still life 'provides proof positive that modern art can aspire to the condition of prayer' (John McEwen, 'My Favourite Painting: Richard Demarco', *Country Life*, 21 October 2009, p. 47).

45. The *Summa Theologica* by Saint Thomas Aquinas, from Aquino in the Ciociaria, is also important to Demarco (BLSA, R5, R34 [accessed 3 March 2021]).

46. Colpi, *Italians' Count*, pp. 121, 129.

47. BLSA, R1, R2, R7 [accessed 19 February 2021].

48. Souir Zekri, '"Real Men Mark their Territory!" Spatial Constructions of Masculinity in Joe Pieri's Autobiographical Narratives', *The European Journal of Life Writing*, 8 (2019), 47–68, (pp. 55–57) and Tom Devine, ed., *Scotland's Shame? Bigotry and Sectarianism in Modern Scotland* (Edinburgh: Mainstream, 2000).

49. Joe Pieri, *Tales of the Savoy: Stories from a Glasgow Café* (Glasgow: Neil Wilson Publishing, 1999), p. 96 and *Gli Italo-Scozzesi. Memorie di un Emigrato* (Lucca: Maria Pacini Fazzi Editore, 2007), pp. 19–20.

50. Cultural Documents, Third Culture, Maison Demarco. Available online: https://www.thirdculture. uk/gallery/maison-demarco/ [accessed 23 September 2021].
51. BLSA, R4; Richard Demarco: The Italian Connection, Launch Event, 30 May 2018. Available online: https://vimeo.com/channels/1377436/280577294 [accessed 12 February 2021].
52. BLSA, R4.
53. BLSA, R2, R3 [accessed 6 February 2021], R7.
54. Smith, 'The Road Goes On', p.11. Demarco has never revealed the names of these 'relations', but recent research confirmed that victim Lorenzo De Marco of Edinburgh was unrelated. (Email correspondence with Laurence Demarco, grandson of victim, February 2021).
55. Lucio Sponza, *Divided Loyalties. Italians in Britain during the Second World War* (Bern: Peter Lang, 2000).
56. For example, Claire Walker, 'Artist, Impresario, Provocateur, Outsider, Prophet: Will the Real Richard Demarco Stand Up?', *The Herald*, 22 Feb 2020. Available online: https://www.heraldscotland.com/news/18254029.artist-impresario-provocateur-outsider-proph et-will-real-richard-demarco-stand/ [accessed 14 February 2021].
57. Terri Colpi, 'Chaff in the Winds of War? The Arandora Star, Not Forgetting and Commemoration at the 80th Anniversary', *Italian Studies*, 75.4 (2020), 389-410.
58. See David McLean, 'Richard Demarco Calls for Edinburgh Memorial to Arandora Star Victims', *Edinburgh Evening News*, 2 Jul 2020. Available online: https://www.edinburghnews. scotsman.com/heritage-and-retro/retro/richard-demarco-calls-for-edinburgh-memorial-arandor a-star-victims-2902230 [accessed 14 February 2021].
59. Demarco recalls being taken to see Fascist propaganda newsreels of the Italian invasion of Abyssinia at Leith Walk's Savoy Theatre in Edinburgh, saying his father attended 'because all his friends were there'. He also recounts his father going to Italy in the 1930s and rowing Corrado Castelvecchi from Largs across to Millport on the island of Cumbrae to avoid internment arrest (BLSA, R4).
60. I most recently discussed the war with Demarco in October 2018 in an interview directed by Susan Michie and filmed by Marco Federici, but was unable to gain new insight. Giles Sutherland similarly reports Demarco's unwillingness to discuss certain phases of his life in any detail, in this case with reference to student days at Edinburgh College of Art and Moray House Teacher Training College, and later his teaching career at Duns Scotus Academy; Sutherland, 'On the Road to Miekle Seggie', pp. 117, 147, 151.
61. Colpi, 'Chaff in the Winds', p. 394.
62. Rachel Haworth and Laura Rorato, 'Memory, Identity and Migrant Generations: Articulating Italianità in Twentieth and Twenty-First Century Northern England', *California Italian Studies*, 9.1 (2019), 1–19 (p. 13).
63. Colpi, *Italians' Count*, p. 147.
64. See Mario Dutto, ed., *The Italians in Scotland: Their Language and their Culture* (Edinburgh: Edinburgh University Press, 1986).
65. Anne Pia, *Language of My Choosing* (Edinburgh: Luath Press, 2017), pp. 59–60, 83–85, writes of recovering her Italian self through Viticuso dialect and later acquisition of standard Italian.
66. Manuela D'Amore, 'Transcultural Identities, Plurilingualism and Gender in Scottish Italian Literary Writing: Ann Marie Di Mambro, Anne Pia and Mary Contini', *Polyphonie* 7/1 (2020) Available online: http://www.polyphonie.at/index.php?op=publicationplatform&sub=viewcontribution&contribut ion=220 [accessed 27 September 2021] and Emanuela Bianchera et al, 'Transnational Mobility and Cross-Border Family Life Cycles: A Century of Welsh-Italian Migration', *Journal of Ethnic and Migration Studies*, 45.16 (2019), 3157 3172, (pp. 3166–3169).
67. See Carla Dente, 'Personal Memory/Cultural Memory: Identity and Difference in Scottish Italian Migrant Theatre' in Manfred Pfister and Ralf Hertel, eds., *Performing National Identity. Anglo-Italian Cultural Transactions* (Rodopi: Amsterdam, 2008), pp. 197–212.
68. For discussion of 'Celtic Italian' identity in Wales, see Liz Wren-Owens, 'The Delayed Emergence of Italian Welsh Narratives, or Class and the Commodification of Ethnicity', *Journal of Migration and Culture*, 3.1 (2012), 119–134 (pp. 125–126).
69. BLSA, R2. In Richard Demarco, *A Life in Pictures* (Ellon: Northern Books, 1995), p.14, Demarco states ' … I am completely at home in Edinburgh in a way I could never be in any Italian city...'.
70. Their journey to Rome included a sojourn in Paris where Carmino pointed out family relations who had been artists' models personified in the statuary of the Place de la Concorde (BLSA, R1). Demarco's first visit to Picinisco was in 1978, as part of an 'Edinburgh Arts' journey (email correspondence with Demarco, January 2021).
71. At St Ninian's Catholic Church, Edinburgh, 27 December 1956, officiated by Demarco's uncle, Father Giovanni Fusco.
72. BLSA, R14 [accessed 24 February 2021].
73. BLSA, R14.
74. Demarco Archive. Richard Demarco Biography. Available online: https://www.demarco-archive.ac.uk/richard_demarco_biography.pdf [accessed 21 June 2021].

75. BLSA, R24 [accessed 1 March 2021]. Demarco cited the Leo Castelli Gallery in New York, founded in 1957, to support using his own name. See also, Richard Demarco: The Italian Connection, interview with Richard Demarco, January 2017. Available online: https://vimeo.com/channels/1377436/280577294 [accessed 20 May 2021].
76. Richard Demarco, 'Too Rough to Go Slow' (unpublished expanded manuscript, 2020), p. 49.
77. In many ways, Demarco's journey can be traced through his name evolutions: Ricardo, known as 'Rico' in family and Italian circles, became 'Ricky' at school, college and in the early days of arts pioneering, transitioning to 'Richard' and more recently returning to Rico again. See Endnote 99.
78. Leuzzi, 'Edimburgo-Roma', p. 207.
79. BLSA, R24.
80. BLSA, R24.
81. Demarco, 'Too Rough To Go Slow', p. 121.
82. Accompanying text to the exhibition 'Richard Demarco, Scotland and Italy in Watercolour' at the Scottish Gallery in 2010 stated 'With my Italo-Scottish cultural heritage, I am deeply aware of the journeys taken by my forebears. … I see them journeying on what I define as "The Road to Meikle Seggie".'
83. Demarco, 'Too Rough To Go Slow', p. 92.
84. NRS death certificates record 1977 for Carmino Demarco and 1985 for Elizabeth Demarco (neé Fusco).
85. Demarco, 'Too Rough to Go Slow', p. 104.
86. Demarco's father and brother, Louis, ran a café in William Street, behind the Demarco Gallery at Melville Crescent, (BLSA, R47 [accessed 5 March 2021). Louis is known to have spent time at the Traverse Theatre (email correspondence with artist Nathan Huxtable, February 2021), and appears in photographs outside the Demarco Gallery. See https://www.demarco-archive.ac.uk/ assets/6050-p1977_louis_demarco_maurice_roeves_john_cairney_high_street_edinburghp/lightbox [accessed 20 February 2021].
87. From a younger generation, Chris Capaldi, born in Edinburgh, personifies the model tradition today, in his case transitioning from modelling into acting.
88. BLSA, R13 [accessed 24 February 2021].
89. Coia's family was from Filignano, 20km from Picinisco in the Molise region.
90. See https://www.demarco-archive.ac.uk/assets/3779-p1973_emilio_coia_drawing_tadeusz_kantor_edinburgh_arts_1973p [accessed 24 August 2021].
91. BLSA, R34, R57, R61 [accessed 6 March 2021]; Richard Demarco, 'Christmas Newsletter', 2020.
92. BLSA, R34; Richard Demarco: The Italian Connection. Available Online: https://www.vimeo.com/channels/1377436/280577294 [accessed 20 May 2021].
93. Derek Duncan, '"The Path that Leads me Home":Eduardo Paolozzi and the Arts of Trans-nationalizing' in Charles Burdett, Loredana Polezzi and Barbara Spadaro, eds., *Transcultural Italies: Mobility, Memory and Translation* (Liverpool, Liverpool University Press, 2020), pp. 127–154, (p. 151).
94. Timothy Neat, *Hamish Henderson: A Biography, Volume 2, Poetry Becomes People, 1952–2002* (Edinburgh: Polygon, 2009), pp. 135–136.
95. See short film 'An Introduction to Art and Healing', Dir., Marco Federici, 2019. Available online: https://www.demarcoarchive.com/art-and-healing-venice-2019 [accessed 24 June 2021].
96. In music, acting and writing, Nicola Benedetti, Paolo Nutini, Lewis Capaldi, Tom Conti, Peter Capaldi, Daniela Nardini, Armando Iannucci, Mary Contini and Ann Marie Di Mambro are just some of the household names.
97. *No-Where-Next | War-Diaspora-Origin*, Cassino (4–6 May 2013). See: https://www.altreitalie.it/la_finestra_di_altreitalie/news/no-where-next__war-diaspora-origin_co nver genze_ed_esplorazioni_di_metodo_intorno_allemigrazione_italiana.kl [accessed 28 July 2021].
98. Descended from both the Chiaverini-McGuinness and Fusco-Brattesani lines, Federici and Demarco are related twice over. Originally from Sheffield, but now living in Glasgow, Federici might conceivably be understood as a family custodian of the Demarco legacy.
99. See award winning film 'Rico – The Richard Demarco Story', Dir., Marco Federici, 2021. Trailer available online: https://www.youtube.com/watch?v=Rt4BHcte9lU [accessed 13 November 2021].
100. Demarco, *The Road to Meikle Seggie*.
101. Luigi Giannetti, *Pastorizia* (Picinisco: Pro Loco, Comune di Picinisco, 2000).
102. For example, an invitation in 2021 from Andrea Cusumano of Palermo to collaborate on a new project linking the European margins of Scotland and Sicily by highlighting the work of Demarco alongside that of Ludovico Corrao who brought international artists to Gibellina, destroyed by earthquake in 1968, turning the town into an open air museum and festival site.

The long 70s: Italian Journeys through the Demarco Archives

Laura Leuzzi

Looking at Post-war Italian Art through the Demarco Archives and Richard's own recollections is like travelling in a time machine through some of the most important and exciting movements, artists and artworks of Italian art of the 20th Century. A key aspect is the sheer variety of art-forms, styles and practices promoted.

One of the earliest exhibitions at the RDG was – in fact – a prestigious exhibition organised in collaboration with the Galleria Nazionale d'Arte Moderna di Roma. The exposition – open between 14th March and 7th April 1967 – would come to be considered a milestone in the Italo-Scottish dialogues initiated and was developed by Demarco.

An early draft of the press release underlined the importance for the newly founded gallery of hosting an event of such importance and resonance that it would 'justify its existence on its own'.[1]

As on many occasions in Demarco's life, the collaboration sprang from an entirely serendipitous coincidence (Figures 1 and 2). In the inaugural days of the RDG in 1966, Giorgio de Marchis – at the time a young *ispettore* (curator) at the National Gallery of Modern Art in Rome (1930–2009),[2] while in Edinburgh for a sculpture exhibition at the National Gallery of Modern Art and the Festival – walked through the doors of the gallery.[3] The encounter marked the start of a professional and personal relationship between the two institutions.[4]

In a letter from Demarco to the then

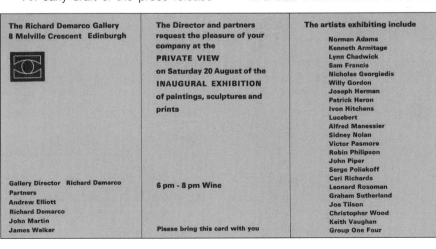

The Richard Demarco Gallery 8 Melville Crescent Edinburgh	The Director and partners request the pleasure of your company at the PRIVATE VIEW on Saturday 20 August of the INAUGURAL EXHIBITION of paintings, sculptures and prints	The artists exhibiting include
		Norman Adams
		Kenneth Armitage
		Lynn Chadwick
		Sam Francis
		Nicholas Georgiadis
		Willy Gordon
		Joseph Herman
		Patrick Heron
		Ivon Hitchens
		Lucebert
		Alfred Manessier
		Sidney Nolan
		Victor Pasmore
		Robin Philipson
		John Piper
		Serge Poliakoff
		Ceri Richards
Gallery Director Richard Demarco	6 pm - 8 pm Wine	Leonard Rosoman
Partners		Graham Sutherland
Andrew Elliott		Joe Tilson
Richard Demarco		Christopher Wood
John Martin	Please bring this card with you	Keith Vaughan
James Walker		Group One Four

Figure 1: *Inaugural Exhibition of Paintings, Sculptures and Prints*, Private View Card, 1966.

25

Figure 2: View of RDG. Inaugural Exhibition. Edinburgh, August–September 1966. Richard Demarco in the RDG, 8 Melville Crescent, Edinburgh, during the Inaugural Exhibition of Paintings, Sculptures and Prints (fifty-three contemporary artists). The large painting is by Michael Tyzack.

largest in Great Britain'. He further argued that the exhibition would contribute significantly to the arts in Edinburgh and offer opportunities for the works exhibited to be acquired by private or public collections.[6]

The exhibition was curated by the *Sovrintendente* of the National Gallery, Palma Bucarelli.[7] It toured in Rome, Dortmund, Cologne, Bergen and Oslo, and thanks to Demarco also went on to Belfast, to Edinburgh and then to the newly founded Oxford Museum of Modern Art.[8]

The Scottish catalogue begins with a brief but very insightful introduction by Bucarelli. The essay – the original Italian typescript for which can be found in the archive – justifies the selection, which at first sight might seem simply a generic group exhibition of Italian Contemporary art. Bucarelli had deliberately excluded the great masters whose works had already been exhibited at the Venice Biennale in earlier years, though there were notable exceptions (Fontana, Burri and Capogrossi among them). 'The sole aim,' Bucarelli declared, '[is to give] an historical perspective into some current artistic movements well connected with their practices'.[9]

The aim was not, therefore, to survey the Italian contemporary art scene, but to illustrate some directions relating to research into it and its development' (in the English translation this was rendered more simply as 'individual experimental developments'). Bucarelli hoped in other words to show 'the direction in which the experiments of the youngest and most advanced artists in Italy are heading today'.[10]

Bucarelli uses the adjective '*indicativa*' (in the English title the term is translated as 'orientative') in order to suggest that the exhibition would try to update the audience on current artistic developments and debates.[11]

Sovrintendente (superintendent) of the National Gallery of Modern Art in Rome, Palma Bucarelli, dated 22nd September 1966, Demarco recalls that de Marchis visited the *Inaugural Exhibition of Paintings, Sculptures and Prints* at the RDG.

As a follow-up, James Walker, a Director of the RDG, went to Rome to discuss the hosting of a contemporary art exhibition in Edinburgh.[5] De Marchis suggested that the RDG could host the exhibition *Contemporary Italian Art*, originally included in the *Semaines Italiennes* at the Municipal Casino of Cannes (12th December 1965 – 2nd January 1966), promoted by the Ente Nazionale Italiano del Turismo and realised by the Galleria Nazionale di Roma. RDG was 'one of the

In my view, the selection itself reflects Bucarelli's refined intelligence and sensibility, evident in the red thread he draws between "historical avant-gardes" and the "current avant-gardes". Indeed, much contemporary criticism and debate had been concerned with precisely this dialogue between these two alignments. Just the year before, in 1966, Maurizio Calvesi had published his famous collection *Le due avanguardie* (The Two Avant-Gardes).[12]

Contemporary Italian Art included works (Figures 3, 4 and 5) by a group of artists who would shortly take part in the renowned exhibitions *Arte Povera* at Galleria La Bertesca in Genoa (1967) and at Galleria de' Foscherari in Bologna (1968): Pino Pascali, Mario Ceroli, Jannis Kounellis. Other movements included the kinetic art of Gruppo T and Nuova Tendenza and Gruppo N (Toni Costa), Nouveau Realisme, as well as representatives from so- called Italian Pop Art (Franco Angeli, Tano Festa, Mimmo Rotella, Mario Schifano and Cesare Tacchi).

At Demarco's instigation, the exhibition was shown in other cities too. Before reaching Edinburgh, it was hosted by the Ulster Museum in Belfast (1st-25th February 1967), whereas afterwards it went on to the "young" Museum of Modern Art in Oxford (25th April – 20th May 1967).[13]

Because of previous commitments at RDG,[14] the artworks could not be displayed in Scotland before March,[15] and the event in Belfast offered an opportunity to keep the works out of storage, to arrange for the onerous transport expenses from Norway to be shared by several galleries, and to further promote Italian art abroad.

Regarding the issue of "restoration work", "no attempt should be made at permanent work but only temporary touching up".

The Edinburgh exhibition also re-

Figure 3 (*upper*): *Contemporary Italian Art*, exhibition cover, 1967.

Figure 4 (*centre*): *Contemporary Italian Art*, exhibition view, 1967. [Courtesy of La Galleria Nazionale d'arte Moderna e Contemporanea, Bio-iconographic Archive, Rome.]

Figure 5 (*lower*): *Contemporary Italian Art*, Museum of Modern Art Oxford, private view card, 27 April 1967.

ceived the prestigious backing of the Ministry of Foreign Affairs, the Italian Embassy in London and from the Italian Consulate General in Edinburgh. In a communication to Demarco, the Italian ambassador to London, Gastone Guidotti, conceives of the event as a golden opportunity to foster the bond between Scotland, and Edinburgh in particular, and Italy.[16]

Surveying the critical reception through the extant press material at the Demarco archives at the SNGMA and at the Archives at the National Gallery of Modern Art in Rome, it appears as though the exhibition met with somewhat mixed reviews. Over the years, Demarco himself has repeatedly recalled the cool reception accorded *Contemporary Italian Art* by Scottish critics.[17]

While the iterations in Cannes, Oslo and Belfast had been welcomed warmly by press and public alike[18], the Edinburgh exhibition did not receive the same level of attention or, indeed, appreciation: for example, the Edinburgh Italian Consul General of the time, Alfredo Trinchieri (1965–67) talks about a 'sour and severe criticism' in a review published in the pages of *The Scotsman* (20th March 1966).[19]

The bitter review referred to by the Consul has the unflattering title *Follies in Dotty Show by Italians* by the art critic, journalist and nationalist poet writing for The Scotsman, Sydney Goodsir Smith (1915–1975).[20]

One might even argue that it was the international character of the exhibition that was not appreciated by Goodsir Smith. According to him, the exhibition, or a large part of it, was nothing but 'an awful lot of tosh and exceedingly pretentious tosh at that'. He then proceeded to produce simplistic and mocking descriptions of the artworks by Francesco Lo Savio *Uniform Matt Black Metal* (original

title: *Metallo nero opaco uniforme*, 1960, 50 x 200 cm), and of *Achrome* (1959, canvas, 82 x 63 cm) by Piero Manzoni, showing that he had simply not understood the poetics of these artists and more generally of contemporary artistic movements. On the other hand, even the descriptions of artworks that in his eyes were of higher quality are reduced to the status of mere gags. The tone is one of underlying sarcasm.

Nevertheless, Goodsir Smith's disparagement was mitigated by a letter addressed to the paper's director by an 'associate of Mr Demarco', the art critic John Martin, which denounced 'the little objectivity of the critic', who had focused on the most marginal and unknown artworks. Trinchieri recounts that the letter was followed by a reply from Goodsir Smith asking contentiously if similar artworks would have been included in an exhibition of Scottish art in Rome.[21]

Conversely, another review appeared in *The Herald*[22] on 23rd March, giving a warmer welcome to "Mrs. Bucarelli's' selection" and emphasising that "the range is wide enough to make it virtually certain that all but the most unrepentant reactionary will find something to [their] taste".[23]

Trinchieri reveals that there was a "lively controversy", to judge by the numerous letters received by the editor of The Scotsman expressing many readers' disappointment at an 'excessively bigoted and dogged' criticism.[24]

Among the positive outcomes highlighted in the report there features a steady, almost uninterrupted flow of visitors ("a daily average of more than 200 people"), guided tours organised by schools and universities, and the subsequent exhibition in Oxford.[25] Moreover, the Italian Consulate in Edinburgh had actively supported the event, mailing several copies of the exhibition press release to members of various Italo-scottish communities across Scotland.[26] Demarco confirmed the successful reception granted the exhibition by the general public in a letter dated 22nd March 1967 to architect Trevor Green, the founder and original director of the Museum of Modern Art in Oxford, by stating that the visitor numbers had surpassed all previous exhibitions.[27] Demarco also wrote in a similar vein to Ford Smith, Keeper of Art at the Ulster Museum, informing him that the exhibition had attracted many visitors and aroused a great deal of interest, including at Oxford.[28] Even if the Edinburgh critics had not responded enthusiastically to the exhibition, audiences for their part had reacted much more positively.

Trinchieri himself recounts in a report to the Ministry that he had personally introduced to the public at the opening, the courageous selection of artworks featuring better and less well-known artists side by side, referencing Bucarelli's statement in the catalogue. Probably anticipating the caustic reaction that would appear in the pages of *The Scotsman* a few days later, Trinchieri reflected 'that some or even many of the visitors will not accept at face value the means and outcomes proposed in the exhibition, but be that as it may, they cannot be ignored as they are tormented, living and strong expressions of the time in which we live'.[29] Another report referencing the article from *The Scotsman* came from the Foreign Ministry – apparently signed by ambassador Guidotti – and notes 'how old Scotland remains almost fully unprepared to welcome artworks that do not retrace the models of the most customary figurative art'.[30]

It is not surprising, therefore, that only one sale occurred during the exhibition at Richard Demarco Gallery. Vivien Gough-Cooper, one of the directors of RDG, who was amassing a small but interesting private collection, acquired *Oggetto Dinamica Visuale, BB 65* (in English *Visual Dynamic, BB65*, wood and plastics, 85 x 85 x5 cm) by Toni Costa (1935-2013), which appeared on the catalogue cover.[31]

Although in the National Gallery of Rome archives there is a letter dated 29 July 1966 in which it is mentioned that Galleria dell'Obelisco has requested the restitution of *BB65*, the work had continued its journey with the rest of the exhibition.[32]

Searching through the documents, in a letter to Bucarelli from Trevor Green, director of Museum of Modern Art in Oxford, we read that the launch of the exhibition went 'very well'.[33] It is natural, then, to ask quite why the exhibition should have met with such hostile a critical reception at the Richard Demarco Gallery in Edinburgh. Possibly, this was a simply a puzzled response to the sheer novelty of a survey of contemporary Italian art introduced into the Scottish context. After all, Trinchieri states in his report that this was the very first exhibition entirely dedicated to Italian contemporary art ever to have been shown in Edinburgh. However, as mentioned above, examining the Scottish art scene of those years, it emerges that the British Council and the Italian Ministero della Pubblica Istruzione had organized an exhibition of Italian sculpture at the Scottish National Gallery of Modern Art a year earlier.[34] The selection entitled *Twenty Italian Sculptors* (13th August – 18th September 1966) – again curated by Bucarelli and wide ranging as to 'ages, approaches and trends' – owed its initial momentum to the interest shown by Douglas Hall, Curator at the Scottish National Gallery of Modern Art, who had promoted the project since 1962.[35]

The Superintendent explains in the

catalogue introduction to the catalogue that the exhibition aims to bear witness to the importance of contemporary Italian sculpture, even within a crisis affecting traditional techniques, as it maintained a strong connection with tradition while focusing on innovation.

The younger artists' more radical practices, which do not often accord with the above description, were given only limited exposure. Among the most important artists in the exhibition – which would also tour Hull, Sheffield, Manchester, Bristol and Coventry – were featured Ettore Colla, Pietro Consagra, Pericle Fazzini, Lucio Fontana, Leoncillo Leonardi, Giacomo Manzù, Umberto Mastroianni, Arnaldo and Gio' Pomodoro, and Alberto Viani.

The Times correspondent in Edinburgh observed that despite the fame of artists like 'Mastroianni, Manzù, Fontana and the brothers Pomodoro', the exhibition represented a unique opportunity for Scotland to finally see their artworks in person and not only in the guise of photographic reproductions. Moreover, according to the same critic, the exhibition's sculptures, displayed in the garden, were complemented by Marino Marini's *Pomona* (1949, bronze, 170 x 80.50 x 58 cm), part of the museum's permanent collection. Marini himself, together with Manzù, is mentioned in Bucarelli's introduction, where note is taken of his established presence in (the) British collections, which had brought some awareness of Italian sculpture to the general public in the United Kingdom.

Various factors contributed to the more positive reception granted to *Twenty Italian Sculptors* when compared to the decidedly cool welcome given to *Contemporary Italian Art*. One hypothesis could be simply that the positive review for the Italian sculpture exhibition by *The Times* correspondent did not fully reflect

the local critics' opinions on contemporary art. Another possibility is that the presentation of *Contemporary Italian Art* in a "young", not wholly established gallery may somehow have led to the negative judgements described above. It is also possible that the selection of already internationally renowned sculptors at the Scottish National Gallery of Modern Art, compared to the younger generation of the artists at the RDG, could have influenced the different judgements.

Although *Contemporary Italian Art* was indeed greeted by mixed reviews, the importance of this exhibition for the RDG should not be underestimated. I believe that the exhibition marked the beginning of a series of profound relationships formed by Demarco, inspiring him to enter into contact and develop correspondences, to foster exchanges and partnerships with a wide range of different Italian institutions, galleries, artists, curators and cultural entrepreneurs.

Furthermore, some traces in the Demarco Archives suggest that he remained in touch over the years, as mentioned above, with de Marchis, with Bucarelli, and with the National Gallery of Modern Art in Rome.[36]

Documentary evidence further suggests that in 1970 Demarco initiated a relationship with the famous Florence Centro Di, to sell RDG publications and catalogues.[37]

In 1970 Demarco was also contacted by Leonardo Magini and Il Nuovo Torcoliere in Via del Babbuino in Rome regarding prints and multiples.[38]

There are also traces of a correspondence with Lucio Amelio's Modern Art Agency in Naples dating from 1972.[39]

Between 1969–70 Demarco develops an intense correspondence with Galleria Vaccarino in via Tornabuoni in Florence.[40] The galleries discuss a possible collaboration, involving the exchange of exhibitions – as mentioned by Demarco in a letter dated 12 March 1970, an exhibition of James Morrison in Florence (although the original plans outlined in letters were dated to Autumn 1969), and one of Bryan Senior in Edinburgh, both opening in October 1970 (October/ November). As a result of this exchange, Senior was included in *Four Figurative Painters* with Patrick Hayman, Will Maclean, and Tony Valentine, an exhibition that was hosted at RDG in October/November 1970.

A key relationship, starting in the late 60s and shaping the RDG's activities in the 70s and 80s, is that with the very famous Venetian Galleria del Cavallino, founded in 1942 by Carlo Cardazzo and latterly co-directed by his children Paolo and Gabriella. Although this partnership has been mentioned in several publications, it has never been explored in depth and its beginnings have been uncovered only by the author of this chapter as part of Richard Demarco: The Italian Connection.[41]

In a letter to Richard Demarco dated 7 January 1968 (more probably dating to 1969) and signed by Paolo Cardazzo, the co-director of Galleria del Cavallino expresses a wish to develop a "cooperation" between the two galleries "following up to our meeting of last Summer".

Gabriella Cardazzo recalls that the encounter was probably fostered by artist Paolo Patelli, who had been with the gallery for some years. Richard had visited the Cavallino Gallery while in town for the Biennale.[42] Demarco replies on February 4th expressing interest in a possible collaboration and sends a number of catalogues with a view to starting a conversation. By way of a reply – after a short break in communications – Cardazzo proposes an exhibition of "joung (young) Italian artists Patelli Perusini Fungenzi ecc (sic)" at the RDG and offers in ex-

change to host an exhibition of "painters" suggested by Demarco.[43]

Richard welcomes this offer with enthusiasm, saying that he is "most interested" and encloses a brochure of the 1969 Edinburgh Festival in which "there is an important exhibition of Italian art". In exchange for information on the Cavallino artists, Demarco would then send slides and biographies of artists who – he feels – "would be most appreciated in Italy". Names include Romanian master Paul Neagu as well as Scottish artists such as Campbell McPhail, Jack Knox, Rory McEwen, James Gavin and group 1-4.[44]

Soon after, Cardazzo sent various artists' slides (a list includes Giorgio Azzaroni, Paolo Patelli, Luciano Celli, Toni Fulgenzi, Romano Perusini), further information and catalogues.[45] In the folder at the Archives can be found the Cavallino catalogues – the distinctive square leaflets – of the artists mentioned.

Demarco was somewhat slow to reply: in a letter dated 23 December he proposes that he organise an exhibition of RDG artists in Italy in Spring 1971, sharing costs with Cavallino. The exhibition would tour from Venice to a number of other locations, including Rome, where Maria Alfani, director of Studio Farnese, was "anxious to see an exhibition of our artists in Rome".[46]

Once again Demarco mentions the name of Paul Neagu as well as Trevor Bell, Michael Tyzack and John Knox. He offers in return to help the exhibition touring in other venues with which he has relationships, including the Museum of Modern Art in Oxford.

Looking at Demarco's proposals, it is interesting to note that Demarco's proposals do not take the form of a thematic or stylistic curatorial project of some kind: the idea is more to have the opportunity to promote the artists and the gal-

Figure 6:: From the left: Paolo Patelli, Gabriella Cardazzo, Igino Legnaghi and Giorgio Teardo. Edinburgh Arts 1974.

lery's activities. The groups do not retain a specific Scottish character, although some Scottish artists are included: what emerges is an openness to a European avantgarde that is a constellation of different styles and languages.

Demarco's proposed plans are then stalled once again: Cardazzo replies only in March offering to discuss the matter in person when Demarco comes to Venice for the Biennale.[47] The two won't meet on that occasion and the dialogue will continue, for the time being by letter and with the exchange of diverse materials.

To judge by this early correspondence, the two galleries shared a strong mutual interest in creating an enduring collaboration. Although there was some delay in realising the various projects that were floated, most of the suggested exhibitions would be developed during the course of the next few years.

Due to a series of untoward circumstances, the collaboration did not bear fruit until the autumn of 1973: in November Demarco organised *4 Venetian artists* in collaboration with Cavallino, an exhibition featuring Anselmo Anselmi, Franco Costalonga, Paolo Patelli and Romano Perusini.

Gabriella Cardazzo, who accompanied the Cavallino artists to Edinburgh, remembers how Demarco organised an

intensive programme of meetings and visits while in town.[48]

Then, in August/September 1974, Demarco hosted *7 Galleria del Cavallino Artists* at *Edinburgh Arts 74*, an exhibition hosted at the Royal College of Physicians that included Legnagni, Sutej, Patelli, Teardo, and formed part of the Edinburgh Arts in August/September (Figures 6 and 7).

From a letter by Demarco dated 28 May 1974, it can be inferred that he was trying to organise other venues for the exhibition to tour. In an undated note preserved at the Cardazzo Archival Collection at the Cini Foundation in Venice, the collaboration between the two galleries is outlined in three steps: the first is the tour of the Cavallino exhibition in the UK (with destinations that include Sheffield School of Art and the Oxford Museum of Modern Art); an "Expedition", which refers to the Edinburgh Arts Summer Programme, schematically summarised as "Malta Mediterranean Megalithic to (Italia Venezia) Renaissance to North Europe (France Holland England) to Scotland Hebrides Celtic Megalithic"; a phase three with a retrospective for Paolo Patelli which, to judge by the available records, was never organised.[49]

Among the correspondence relating to the organisation of *7 Galleria del Cavallino Artists*, there is an interesting letter from Gabriella Cardazzo to Demarco, not dated, in which the Venetian gallerist explains that – although she had not yet received confirmation from the RDG, – she had already invited Legnaghi. This artist, she explained, had been working on a piece especially for the Festival featuring an IBM computer and if space was lacking, she would have preferred to drop other artists in order to accommodate him.[50] Although not with the artwork mentioned in the original proposal, one of Legnaghi's pieces was ultimately included in the final exhibition. In the Cardazzo Archival Collection at the Cini Foundation in Venice, there is a typewritten copy of the list of the artworks that were in deposit at the RDG in Edinburgh for the Edinburgh Arts exhibition with details and prices:[51] under Legnaghi's name we can find two anodised aluminium plates, but no trace at all of the computer art piece mentioned by Gabriella in the earlier correspondence. It may have been cancelled for technical reasons and on grounds of economy.

Gabriella Cardazzo and the Cavallino artists have expressed their gratitude on several different occasions for Demarco's warm welcome. In the SNGMA Archive, there can be found a heartfelt thank you note from Anselmi to Demarco, in which he explains that he was "happy to have the possibility to come to Edinburgh in a particular standstill time for me and to get some new outlooks for my work". In this short passage, Anselmi's words reveal the importance of the artists' visits facilitated by Demarco: a source of inspiration and opportunity.[52]

Later that same year Cavallino would finally host the first exhibition from Scotland, in collaboration with the RDG: *John Knox, Iain Patterson, Ainslie Yule* (26 September – 25 October 1974) (Figures 8 and 9).

In the documents at the SNGMA Archive, it is interesting to note that Demarco had initially invited Ian Hamilton Finlay to show his work at Cavallino. This would have been Finlay's very first exhibition in Italy. In a letter dated 28 November 1973, Finlay apologises for not being able to welcome some Italian guests (probably Gabriella Cardazzo and the Cavallino artists who were exhibiting and who had accompanied her), due to poor health and the need to attend to various works in his gallery. He also adds: "as

regards the Italian exhibition, will the other two be showing works which go on the walls?" If so, he would plan to do something that would "pack flat" and go in the middle of the room.[53]

Despite this early correspondence, Finlay's place was later taken by Ainslie Yule, who had recently exhibited at the Whitechapel Gallery in London.[54]

In the essay for the exhibition catalogue (of which a typewritten English version exists in the Fondo Cardazzo at the Cini Foundation), Demarco underlines the importance of fostering Italo-Scottish cultural relationships for his own "heritage" but he also reminds the reader of an historic connection between the two countries with the tradition of Scottish artists visiting Italy in the 18th and 19th

Figure 7: Edinburgh Arts 1974 (19 July – 7 September 1974), exhibition catalogue: page dedicated to Igino Legnaghi Paolo Patelli.

Figure 8 (*upper*): *John Knox, Iain Patterson, Ainslie Yule*, exhibition view, 26 September – 25 October 1974. On the left: Ziva Kraus.

Figure 9 (*lower*): Exhibition *John Knox, Iain Patterson, Ainslie Yule*, 26 September – 25 October 1974 view of the exhibition. On the walls paintings by Iain Patterson. On the floor sculpture by Ainslie Yule.

century as part of their Grand Tour. One very renowned example that certainly comes to mind is the Scottish Neoclassical painter Gavin Hamilton (1723–1798).

Demarco talks about the key presence of the Italian community in Scotland and even suggests that the visual arts might provide a clue as to why Italians tended to prefer Scotland to England for their immigration.

This cultural dialogue might bear particular fruits in "this time when too many artists are dominated by what has come to be known as International style". In Demarco's opinion Yule, Pattison and Knox's works share a quintessentially Scottish character: "a poetic view of space and time". He links this exhibition to the 1967 *Contemporary Italian Art* exhibition, saying that he had planned ever

since that moment to have a Scottish exhibition in Italy, and explains how a common understanding shared with Cavallino had made that possible.

After the Venice exhibition, a tour was arranged in partner galleries in the North of Italy, in Vicenza (Ghelfi Gallery), Padua and La Spezia. As a result of this exhibition and tour a number of sales were made.

In 1975 the Edinburgh Arts Summer School was entitled *To Callanish from Hagar Qim*, evoking a journey – which was metaphorically and spiritually forging a connection with the Mediterranean region – represented by the megalithic temple of Hagar Qim in Malta – to the Outer Hebrides – with the Callanish Standing Stones on the Isle of Lewis.

The journey was arranged in two parts: one in Malta and Italy, one in Scotland and England.

In a typewritten document entitled "Edinburgh Arts 1975 Proposed Structure" – which Demarco redrafted for his introduction to the *From Callanish to Hagar Qim* catalogue – it is suggested that a particular value should be put on 'the idea of a journey' that was 'implicit within its structure since the beginning', evoking the spirit of "a pilgrimage and the adventure of an odyssey". Shifting the focus from Edinburgh, the festival and the exhibition, the 1975 edition was therefore to be 'an art expedition'.

The importance of the megalithic sites is to be viewed in the context of the theories that interpreted them as 'Lunar Observatories' as discussed by Prof. Alexander Thom in a lecture at the Royal Society the year before. Sites such as Callanish and Hagar Qim were thus held to represent a harmonic connection with Nature and its rhythms fostered in ancestral times. The students – especially the Americans – would have benefited from uncovering an unusual Europe, in a sort of 'contemporary form of the European "Grand Tour"', one that would not coincide with the stereotype of the Renaissance and would rather bring to light the Celts and the prehistoric era.[55]

A somewhat modified version of this same text changed was then published in the catalogue of the Edinburgh Arts.

The journey – in the days that preceded the opening of the Festival – would include the Road to Meikle Seggie, Iona, and a trip to Sheffield, with a collaboration with the School of Art of the Sheffield Polytechnic, and a visit to stone circles at Harthill Moor, Eyam Moor and Morscar Moor.

Some of the participants would start their journey four weeks prior to the Edinburgh Festival 75 in a sort of "prelude" in Malta where an exhibition at the National Museum featuring local artists and artists from Italy (Cavallino) and Yugoslavia was held.[56]

The group would be composed of a "nucleus" in a "teaching capacity" "who will document the experience with the written words, photography, film and video" and visual artists, dancers and musicians. After the first week in Malta, starting on 13th June, a "pattern" for subsequent legs of the journey would be established.[57] Although photographs taken in Malta show that actions and events were videotaped (with a porta-pack possibly provided by Cavallino, which had begun video art production on a significant scale in 1974 on the initiative of Paolo, who although invited was in the end not able to take part in the journey) and video interviews were conducted. Unfortunately, none of the video recordings have as yet been found.

In this part of the summer school, participants visited the site of Hagar Qim and St. Joseph's Parish Church in Manikata. A photograph shows Cavallino artist Paolo Patelli, explaining his land art piece in front of a camera: the work consists of a long white line against a black background and ending in a block of cement. The spirit of this ongoing creative workshop is well represented in a photograph that shows a quick sketch signed by Anselmo Anselmi on the wall of St. Joseph's Parish Church (Figure 10).

One of the Venetian participants, artist Guido Sartorelli (1936–2016) invited via Gabriella Cardazzo – subsequently made the artwork *Malta rational thinking*, which he later described as follows: "That work on Malta gave a first shape to my possible future" (Figure 11).

Other artists invited include Luciano Fabro, whom Demarco planned to meet on a trip to Milan, in the offices of the art magazine *Flash Art* in May 1975.[58]

On Friday 20 June the group left for Rome, where they visited the National Gallery, and then went on a trip to Central Italy which included Spoleto, Urbino, Assisi, and Arezzo. A map in the Edinburgh Arts catalogue details the tour. They then headed for Florence where – as the programme stated – they would visit the famous Centro Di. Another Florentine collaboration was with Galleria Schema, whose co-founder Alberto Moretti (1922–2012) gave a lecture to the participants at the gallery and was then invited to Edinburgh. A page from the catalogue

Figure 10: Guido Sartorelli, video interview, Malta, Edinburgh Arts 1975.

documents the works by Moretti himself using raffia and straw – inspired by the typical artisanal products of his birthplace Carmignano[59] – entitled *Techne e Lavoro come Arte* [Technique and Work as Art] exhibited in June 1975 at Schema, engaging with the value and dignity of work, and with the respect there should be for work as art.

On the same trip they also visited the art/tapes/22 video art centre, directed and founded by Maria Gloria Bicocchi. Although initially Bicocchi had hoped to participate in most of the 'European Tour' in Malta and Italy,[60] in a telegram dated 3 June 1975, Bicocchi says that she was unable to join the trip but would 'wait for [the] participant(s) in Florence'.[61]

Figure 11: Patelli, Installation and video shoot, Manikata, Malta, Edinburgh Arts 1975.

There the participants attended a workshop by Bill Viola who at the time was employed as an assistant and was working on his early video artworks at art/tapes/22 (Figure 12). From the available photo documentation, it is clear that participants had the rare opportunity to view various video artworks by art/tapes/22 artists. This included a work by Allan Kaprow entitled *Third routine*, in which Andrea Daninos and Lesley Pinnock (Bicocchi's assistant) participated.

At the time art/tapes/22 had achieved international notoriety through the travelling exhibition *Americans in Florence, Europeans in Florence*, and was one of the most important video art centres on this side of the Atlantic.

In a letter from Clare Street to Maria Gloria Bicocchi, she thanks her for the exquisite organisation and hospitality, and she reiterates that, as Richard had suggested, Bicocchi is invited from 20 to 24 August to the Edinburgh Arts, when there could well be an opportunity to show three of the art/tapes/22 videos: Andrea Daninos' *Everybody's Death*, *Suono* [Sound] by Giuseppe Chiari and *Documentary [n. 2]* by Vincenzo Agnetti. Street further explains that RDG would be delighted to become the distributor for art/tapes/22 in Great Britain, and invites Bicocchi to the Edinburgh Arts.[63]

Street likewise writes a personal letter to Bill Viola, thanking him again for the visit at art/tapes/22 and also suggests that – although not for the upcoming Edinburgh Arts show – RDG would be interested in buying his "tape". In those years at art/tapes/22 Viola had made thirteen works of his own, but from this letter it is impossible to decide which one he meant to sell to Demarco.

Unfortunately, neither the tapes, nor Bicocchi, nor indeed Viola would ever make it to the Edinburgh Arts. For, as Bicocchi herself explained in a letter dated 3 September 1975, upon her return from a series of trips, she had discovered that due to various changes in Bill Viola's travel plans, the expedition had not been arranged. She suggests that an exhibition could be organised in the future, nonetheless, and includes the two catalogues of video tapes produced and in deposit at art/tapes/22 with details of editions, two price lists for rentals and sales, and the equivalent listings for the films, records and slides (a new section that in Bicocchi's projects would expand in the future, although it was never developed fully).

In a short reply dated 18 September 1975, Demarco expresses his regret that Bicocchi could not attend the festival and that the tapes were not sent but does mention further opportunities to collaborate in the future.[63]

This missed exhibition could well have been a milestone in the history of the distribution and promotion of Italian video art. Possibly due to the premature ending of art/tapes/22, these opportunities never resulted in a tangible collaboration,

Among the artists mentioned in relation to art/tapes/22 there is the prominent Fluxus member Giuseppe Chiari to whom, in Demarco's recollection, he had first been introduced by Panza di Biumo. In an undated handwritten note, near to Chiari's name there appear two entries, which could be occasions on which Demarco had planned to meet the artist: Art/tapes 30 June; Cavallino 3-4 July.[64] Although not through art/tapes/22, Chiari nonetheless was exhibited at the Edinburgh Arts with a different work: a version of *ART IN EASY* (197) from the *Statement series*.

This motto was at the heart of Chiari's thought and approach and is a simple and direct hymn to the fact that art is open to everybody, and everybody can become an artist. This reflection on the power of creativity and the figure of the artist – which can be accessed by anyone – resonates profoundly with Demarco's approach within the Edinburgh Arts and the RDG.

Reverting now to analysing the tour, after Florence, the group then moved to the north, to reach Venice and visit Cavallino and stay in Stra near Venice where Luigino Rossi – collector and friend of the Cardazzos – had his villa with his renowned collection – Villa Fos-

Figure 12: Bill Viola lecturing the participants of Edinburgh Arts 1975, art/tapes/22, Florence.

carini Rossi that is today Museo Rossi-moda della calzatura and open to the public.

Among the activities scheduled in Venice, a letter dated 12 May 1975 from Clare Street to Ripa Di Meana, at the time Director of the Venice Biennale, proposes a meeting with the Edinburgh Arts participants.

From Venice a trip to Motovun was also organised on July 6: there a meeting with 14 Yugoslav artists took place.[65]

In a typewritten draft of the Edinburgh Arts catalogue preserved in the archives, Demarco explains that he had originally planned to organise a symposium in Motovun with those Yugoslav artists who would participate in Aspect 75. The event was to have the same theme as the subsequent Edinburgh symposium: "the significance of the Celtic word ROSC (meaning 'the poetry of vision') in our 20th Century world of art in relation to the experience of the 'Edinburgh Arts' as a rethink of exhibition or gallery space and art education".[66] From the documentation available (including a page from the catalogue with the artists' signatures), it seems the event in Motovun was reframed as "a dialogue" between the 19 Edinburgh Arts participants, some of the most important Yugoslav artists of the time and curator Marijan Susovski.

The group also visits Milan where there is collaboration with the Valsecchi Gallery, and then pays a visit to the Panza di Biumo collection in Varese.

The last leg of the tour would take place in Scotland. In Demarco's view, a key event within the programme was a symposium at Monteith House, scheduled for the 23rd and 24th August, entitled *From Callanish to Edinburgh Festival*, which involved Scottish and international speakers, including Italians, in the realm of the visual arts and the computer sec-

tors. Among the most important figures to be invited, to judge by a provisional list of speakers preserved in the archives, were *Flash Art*'s editor Giancarlo Politi – who had been introduced to Demarco by artist Cioni Carpi – and the famous art critic Achille Bonito Oliva – who had introduced an event at the Incontri Internazionali d'arte in Rome on 27 June 1975, entitled *Dallo spazio di Hagar Qim via Roma a Callanish*.[67] Neither of the two would in the end participate in the event, the only Italian speakers being Gabriella Cardazzo and architect Carlo Pezzoni.

In a letter to the speakers, Demarco explains that the speakers had been invited to consider the following issues: 'Why the artist seems to have no proper place in society: Why our education systems, particularly secondary school and universities have no real interest in visual education: Why most artists' festivals and manifestations of art are dominated by music and dramatic arts'. The sessions' title dealt with Celtic culture, the site of Callanish, 'Education through the Visual Arts to counter widespread visual illiteracy and the uses of 20th century media (video computers)' and the expressive and spiritual powers of the arts.[68]

Demarco aimed to engage with systemic issues, stimulating a debate regarding the role of the artist within society, the marginalisation of visual arts within education, and the benefits of incorporating new technologies.

The exhibition for the Edinburgh Arts 1975 included several Italian Cavallino artists, some of whom had participated in the European tour.

One example is Guido Sartorelli, who exhibited and joined the group in Malta, and exhibited work at the Edinburgh Arts. Sartorelli made the artwork *Malta rational thinking*, which he later described as follows: "That work inspired by Malta laid the foundation to my possible future work and it was associated with the very strong interest, sometimes obsessive, that I have always had for the City".[69]

Sartorelli visited Edinburgh several times at Demarco's invitation, and the city came to be at the centre of his work *Ipotesi di lettura urbana – Edimburgo* [Hypothesis of Urban reading – Edinburgh] from 1979.

The Cavallino artist Mario "Piccolo" Sillani Djerrahian also joined the Scottish leg of the tour and exhibited at the Edinburgh Arts: his *Capa* (1973) a conceptual, visual exploration of Robert Capa's famous D-Day landings photograph of the US soldiers' assault on Omaha Beach.

During a trip to Callanish a photograph – taken that day by Gabriella – led to the work *Callanish* (part of the Fotografemi series), where the artist visually and conceptually explored the image

through repetition, seriality and the process of re-photographing photographs (Figures 13, 14 and 15).

Through Cavallino, Edinburgh Arts also hosts the Milanese artist Remo Bianco (1922–1988) who utilises his signature element, the *tableau dorée* – the golden grid – on flags that were carried in a performance through the streets of Edinburgh (Figure 16). This performance can be contexualised as part of his *Appropriazioni* (Appropriations) performance series, such as the one at La Coupole in Paris.[70] The grid – which Rosalind Krauss has identified as one of the marks of Modernity[71] – was a heraldic element for Bianco, who placed it in paintings, performances and installations on existing objects and materials with the idea of making a truly elementary art.

Through the performance, which involved marching through the streets, the artist makes an *appropriazione*, appro-

Figure 13: Mario 'Piccolo' Sillani Djerrahian – Capa (Photo's photo sewed), 1973, photo on canvas, 150×180 cm, Richard Demarco Gallery, Edinburgh 1975. Coll. Galleria del Cavallino, Venice. [Courtesy the artist.]

priation, of the city. As part of the work at the Edinburgh Arts, the flags were installed in the exhibition.

At the Edinburgh Arts Demarco invites also Yervant Gianikian e La Rose, presenting their "Viaggio immaginario da Malta alle Ebridi di Gianikian e La Rose – Agosto 1975".

Among the artists invited to participate in the tour, there was also Cioni Carpi (1923–2011), whom Demarco had met on a previous occasion in Italy through Panza di Biumo.[72] In a letter dated 14 May 1975, signed by Clare

Figure 14: Mario 'Piccolo' Sillani Djerrahian – Callanish, 1975-76, 72 polaroids on balsa-wood painted, 8.6×10.7 cm each, Fruitmarket – Richard Demarco Gallery, Edinburgh 1978. [Courtesy the artist.]

Street, Demarco offers to exhibit *We have created atypical systems* (in Italian *Abbiamo creato atipici sistemi*, 1963–74) in Malta, and at various other venues, including the Edinburgh Festival.[73]

We have created atypical systems is one of the nine works by Cioni Carpi in the Panza di Biumo Collection and is composed of six photographs that document a performance from 1963 in which the artist – facing the viewer – put layer upon layer of clothes on his body while at the same time the pile of books on his lap decrease until, in the final image,

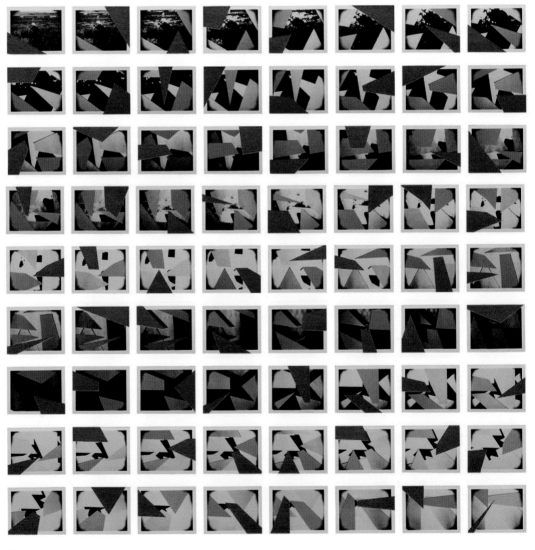

there are no books left. In a text of three pages accompanying the images, Carpi engages with a critique of systems of power and institutions: "The word order, great master, nobody will ever be able to help me, nor world order, nor systems nor philosophy nor art nor adequate truths nor new institutions, only my present, I, here, in this instant, I didn't exist before, I won't after".

Although Carpi did not participate in the Italian leg of the journey, one of his works was included in the Edinburgh Arts exhibition: the page devoted to him in the *From Callanish to Hagar Qim* catalogue

Figure 15 (*upper right*): Trip to Edinburgh on the occasion of Edinburgh Arts, 1975. In the photo Sillani pictured right, Guido Sartorelli on the left, Richard Demarco Gallery, 1975. [Photo by Mario 'Piccolo' Sillani Djerrahian.]
[Courtesy the artist.]

Figure 16 (*lower right*): Remo Bianco, Edinburgh Arts 1975, performance, 30 August 1975]

Figure 17 (*below*): Cioni Carpi, *Trasfigurazione/Sparizione Due*, 1966/1974, Panza Collection, Mendrisio (CH).
[Photo credit Alessandro Zambianchi, Milano / Photo courtesy Panza Collection, Mendrisio (CH)]

features *Trasfigurazione/Sparizione Due* (1966/1974) (Figure 17, another photographic series that documents an action from 1966, accompanied by a text that is reproduced on the same page.[74] The piece documents the artist covering himself with a drape and by reduction arrives almost at annihilation, engaging with concepts of the relation between the subject and external reality.

This artwork is also in the Panza Collection which had loaned the work. As mentioned, the friendship with Panza is longstanding and in the catalogue documenting the 1975 Edinburgh Arts, Panza wrote a brief but significant piece on the Environmental Museum discussing post-war American art. Demarco will promote the Panza collection in Scotland over the years, with presentations and exhibitions.

The 1976 Edinburgh Arts Summer School offered once again the opportunity to travel across Europe. As recorded in a map at the beginning of the catalogue,[75] this time the journey included a leg in Sardinia, to once again create a guiding thread connecting prehistoric sites by exploring the *nuraghe* and other prehistoric structures, including the archaeological site of Su Nuraxi in Barumini and Nuraghe Losa near Abbasanta.

Many other destinations in Italy were reached, including: Pescara, where the Edinburgh Arts participants visited an exhibition of Mario Merz at the newly established Mario Pieroni gallery; Milan where they visited Galleria Valsecchi and the exhibition *Navigazione in Solitario* by Gianfranco Baruchello and the studio of Carlo Pezzoni.

In the following years Demarco continued to nurture his exchanges with Italy and in particular with Cavallino, which led to highly significant exhibitions including in 1983 *Sei Artisti Scozzesi* (Six Scottish Artists) at Galleria del Cavallino, and the following year an exhibition of Gianfranco Venuto at RDG.

In conclusion the 1967 *Contemporary Italian Art* exhibition seems to have been a source of profound inspiration for Demarco, leading him to pursue an Italian connection that was seminal for the development of the activities of the gallery in the 70s and the following decades, Through these relationships – as well as other exchanges with other countries, Demarco managed to open up the activities of his gallery to the European Avant-garde, incorporating different artforms and different approaches and sensibilities. The relationships with the Italian galleries, curators, artists and institutions served to nurture RDG's activities, within conceptual art, performance, and media in particular.

Endnotes

1. Undated annotated typescript. Scottish National Gallery of Modern Art Archive, GMA A37/1/0158. The research on this exhibition has been previously published in: L. Leuzzi, 'Edimburgo-Roma 1967, connessioni italo-scozzesi sulle tracce della mostra Contemporary Italian Art alla Richard Demarco Gallery', *Storia dell'arte*, 2019, n. 1–2, pp. 205–215.
2. He became *sovrintendente* – superintendent – later between 1978 and 1982.
3. A telegram of 12th August 1966 from de Marchis to Douglas Hall, keeper of the Scottish National Gallery of Modern Art in Edinburgh shows that de Marchis stayed in Edinburgh for four nights from 16th August for the exhibition *Twenty Italian Sculptors*. Scottish National Gallery of Modern Art Archive, GMA A33/1/2/32, recto and verso. Referencing Demarco's recollection, de Marchis could visited RDG for a private preview of the *Inaugural Exhibition of Paintings, Sculptures and Prints* at 8 Melville Crescent, which included artworks by 53 artists. The exhibition officially at the rear of the room front left (looking from Cowan Street) opened on 20th August.

4.   In de Marchis' archive are present, in fact, a number of tickets, leaflets and information materials sent by Demarco to announce the exhibitions at RDG between 71 e 74. In a letter of 22nd April 1974, Demarco mentions that he attached several RDG exhibition catalogues for the Gallery library, hopes that he will meet de Marchis and Bucarelli, and thanks him for his participation to a festival in Glasgow. Fondazione Giorgio de Marchis Bonanni d'Ocre Onlus – L'Aquila, Fondo "Raccolta Giorgio de Marchis Bonanni d'Ocre. Documenti di arte contemporanea", Sezione: Mostre collettive. Estero/Gran Bretagna/ Edimburgo, bundle "Galleria Richard Demarco". Thanks go to Fondazione Giorgio de Marchis Bonanni d'Ocre Onlus for their support with this research. Letter from Georges Reymond to Palma Bucarelli of 18th December 1965. Galleria Nazionale d'Arte Moderna, POS. 9B Mostre fuori galleria 1965–1967, Bundle 13, Subfile 1/4873, 18th December 1965.
5.   Scottish National Gallery of Modern Art Archive, GMA A37/1/0157. In a letter from Demarco to de Marchis he stresses: 'I am so pleased you were able to see my partner, Mr Walker, when he was in Rome a fortnight ago'. Further confirmation of this process can be found in a letter of 13th September 1966, in which de Marchis includes a handwritten side note encouraging Demarco to ask Bucarelli to tour the exhibition to Edinburgh, followed by Demarco's answer of 22nd September 1966. SNGMA Archive, GMA A3/1/0157.
6.   Demarco's letter to Bucarelli, 22nd September 1967, SNGMA Archive, GMA A37/1/0157.
7.   Georges Reymond's letter to Palma Bucarelli of 18 December 1965. Galleria Nazionale d'arte moderna e contemporanea (GN), Archivio Storico, POS. 9B Mostre fuori galleria 1965-1967, Bundle 13, Subfile 1/4873, 18 December 1965.
8.   Exhibitions in other venues in Budapest will not take place for a variety of reasons.
9.   The original typescript in Italian can be found in Scottish National Gallery of Modern Art Archive, GMA A37/1/0157. For the revised and edited English translation: Palma Bucarelli in *Contemporary Italian Art*, exhibition catalogue (Belfast, Ulster Museum Art Gallery, 3rd – 25th February 1967; Edinburgh, The Richard Demarco Gallery, 14th March – 7th April 1967), The Richard Demarco Gallery, February/March, catalogue n. 6, 1967, no page numbers. SNGMA Archive, GMA A37/4/03/05.
10. *Ibidem*, author's translation.
11. SNGMA Archive, GMA A37/1/0157.
12. Maurizio Calvesi, *Le due avanguardie* (Milan: Lerici Editore, Milano, 1966; Bari-Roma: Laterza, 1998).
13. Several documents confirm Demarco's mediation. See for example SNGMA Archive, GMA A37/1/0157.
14. Letter from Palma Bucarelli to Richard Demarco, 3rd December 1966, SNGMA Archive, GMA A37/1/0157.
15. Telespresso 1202/687, of 8th December 1966, from the Italian Embassy in Norway addressed to Ministero degli Affari Esteri, to Ministero della Pubblica Istruzione and to Galleria Nazionale. Soprintendenza alla Galleria Nazionale d'Arte Moderna e Contemporanea di Roma – GN, Archivio Storico, POS. 9B Mostre fuori galleria 1965–1967, Bundle 13, Subfile 3/5254
16. Letter from G. Guidotti to Richard Demarco, 17th February 1967. SNGMA Archive, GMA A37/1/0158.
17. See, for example, Bucarelli's statements about the exhibition's need for the support of official entities. SNGMA Archive, GMA A37/1/0157.
18. In a letter to Georges Reymond of 3rd February 1966, de Marchis recounts: 'I'm glad to hear about the success of the exhibition, which has been followed with interest also in Italy', requesting press reviews and catalogues. Galleria Nazionale d'Arte Moderna, Archivio Storico, POS 9/B, Mostre fuori galleria 1965–1967, Bundle 13, Subfile 1/217, 3 febbraio 1966.
     In an unsigned letter addressed to Ministero degli Affari Esteri of 19th November 1966: 'the exhibition closed in Oslo on 6th of this month with great success'. GN, Archivio storico, POS. 9B Mostre fuori galleria 1965–1967, Bundle 13, Subfile 3/4676.
     On the other hand, responses to the exhibition in Belfast had been utterly positive: James W. Ford Smith, Keeper of Art of the Ulster Museum di Belfast, declared it a success, to the point of being sorry that it was coming to an end, and the catalogue was almost sold out. (only 25 remaining copies were sent back to Edinburgh). J. W. Ford Smith's letter to Richard Demarco, 23rd February 1967 and J. W. Ford Smith's letter to Christine Blackwood – Gallery Manager RDG, 2 March 1967. SNGMA Archive, GMA A37/1/0158.
19. Report n. 443/815 dated 30/03/1967, signed by Alfredo Trinchieri, Consolato Generale d'Italia, to the Direzione Generale Relazioni Culturali. GN, Archivio Storico, POS. 9B Mostre fuori galleria 1965–1967, Bundle 13, Subfile 4.
20. Sydney Goodsir Smith, 'Follies in Dotty Show by Italians', *Scotsman*, 20 March 1967.
21. See note 14.
22. 'Contemporary Italian work on Show in Edinburgh', *The Herald* 23 March 1967, 1548.
23. *Ibidem*. Another positive critical opinion is offered by the Italo-Scot journalist Irma Gaddi. Letter by Richard Demarco to Irma Gaddi, 28th April 1967. Scottish National Gallery of Modern Art Archive, GMA A37/1/0158 Italian Contemporary Arts.
24. Report n. 443/815 datato 30/03/1967, signed by Alfredo Trinchieri, Consolato Generale d'Italia, to

the Direzione Generale Relazioni Culturali. Galleria Nazionale d'Arte Moderna, Archivio Storico, POS. 9B Mostre fuori galleria 1965–1967, Bundle 13, Subfile 4.

25. *Ibidem*.
26. See also SNGMA Archive, GMA A37/1/0156. For the Italo-Scottish addresses see also GMA A37/1/0157. ·
27. SNGMA Archive, GMA A37/1/0158.
28. Letter by Richard Demarco to J.W. Ford Smith, 17 March 1967. SNGMA Archive, GMA A37/a/0158 Italian Contemporary Arts.
29. Report n. 399 from the Italian General Consulate in Edinburgh to the Ministry of Foreign Affairs, dated 15/3/1967. GN, Archivio Storico, POS. 9B Mostre fuori galleria 1965–1967, Bundle 13, Subfile 4/1185.
30. Report n. 182/171 of 7th April 1967. GN, Archivio Storico, POS. 9B Mostre fuori galleria 1965–1967, Bundle 13, Subfile 4/1186.
31. Apparently, the artwork – with a declared value of 350.000 Italian lire – was sold by Demarco and paid directly to the artist. The sale is announced and documented several times in the correspondence available. In a letter dated 9th May 1967, Toni Costa communicates to Richard Demarco that Bucarelli informed him of the sale. On 17th May 1967, Demarco confirms to Costa that the artwork has been sold to a 'very close friend of the gallery' (the name is not specified) with a 10% discount and invites him to hold a solo exhibition at RDG (which will not take place). The artist would be entitled to an income of 180.000 Italian lire. A letter of the company Tartaglia to Demarco of 29th August 1967 mentions the identity of the buyer. SNGMA Archive,, GMA A37/1/0158 Italian Contemporary Arts. See also the letter from Palma Bucarelli to Banca d'Italia, 12th April 1968. GN, Archivio Storico, POS. 9B Mostre fuori galleria 1965-1967, Bundle 13, Subfile 3/4975, Corrispondenza Varie. A recent passage of the artwork in an auction is documented at: https://www. invaluable.com/auction-lot/toni-costa-italian-1935-oggetto-dinamica-vis-2067-c-da510f368b (last accessed 20th May 2019).
32. GN, Archivio Storico, POS. 9B Mostre fuori galleria 1965–1967, Bundle 13, Subfile 3/2935
33. Before Green's letter, Demarco wrote to Bucarelli on 29th April 1967 to reassure her that the exhibition was going well. Scottish National Gallery of Modern Art Archive, GMA A37/1/0156 Italian Contemporary Arts. See also a letter from Trevor Green to Palma Bucarelli, dated 3 maggio 1967. GN, Archivio Storico, POS. 9B Mostre fuori galleria 1965–1967, Bundle 13, Subfile 4/1947.
34. See for example the review 'Vigorous Sculpture from Italy', *Times*, 15th August 1966.
35. See documents in the SNGMA Archive, GMA A33/1/2/32.
36. For example, there is a copy of an invitation of the exhibition Piero Manzoni (1933-1963) held at the National Gallery of Modern Art in Rome in February 1971 sent from Palma Bucarelli and in reply a letter dated 13 April 1971 from Richard Demarco to Bucarelli in which he says he is sending a copy of *Strategy gets Art* and asks for a catalogue of the Manzoni exhibition. SNGMA Archive GMA A37/1/0174.
37. A request of copies and information from Centro DI dates to 11 October 1970 to which Demarco replies on 16 November 1970 sending copies and an outline for a commercial agreement. SNGMA Archive, GMA A37/1/0174.
38. Letter from Leonardo Magini to Richard Demarco, dated 10/10 1970, in *Ibidem*.
39. SNGMA Archive, GMA A37/1/0174.
40. SNGMA Archive, GMA A37/1/0449.
41. L. Leuzzi, 'Il talento e la sorte. Il talento e la sorte. La liaison Edimburgo-Venezia dell'Italian Connection di Richard Demarco', *Engramma*, n. 162, 2019.
42. That would be confirmed by the fact the Cavallino copy of the letter, currently in the Cini Archives, which is accompanied by Demarco's card with "Patelli" handwritten on it. See also L. Leuzzi, Interview with Gabriella Cardazzo, September 2017, https://italian. demarco-archive.ac.uk/ 2018/05/24/gabriella-cardazzo/
43. Letter from Richard Demarco to Paolo Cardazzo, 4 February 1969; Letter from P. Cardazzo to Demarco, 2 May 1969, SNGMA Archive A37/1/0174.
44. Letter from Richard Demarco, 8 May 1969, SNGMA Archive A37/1/0174.
45. Letter from Paolo Cardazzo to Richard Demarco, 9 June 1969, SNGMA Archive, GMA A37/1/0174.
46. Letter from Richard Demarco to Paolo Cardazzo, 23 December 1969, SNGMA Archive, GMA A37/1/0174.
47. Letter from Paolo Cardazzo to Richard Demarco, 9 March 1970. SNGMA Archive, GMA A37/1/0174.
48. Interview to Gabriella Cardazzo, Venice, September 2017. Available from https://italian.demarco-archive.ac.uk/2018/05/24/gabriella-cardazzo/. ·
49. Fondazione Cini, Venice, Fondo Cardazzo, Mostra 800.
50. Letter from Gabriella Cardazzo to Richard Demarco, not dated, SNGMA Archive, A37/2/84/9.
51. Fondazione Cini, Venice, Fondo Cardazzo, Mostra 800.
52. Letter from Anselmo Anselmi to Demarco, 24 August 1974, SNGMA Archive, A37/2/84/9. In the same folder a reply from Demarco dates to 9 September 1974.

53. SNGMA Archive, GMA A37/1/1/659.
54. Letter from Anne Goring to Gabriella Cardazzo, Edinburgh, 13 May 1974, SNGMA Archive, GMA A37/2/84/9.
55. See SNGMA Archive, GMA A37/2/105/5.
56. *Ibidem*.
57. *Ibidem*.
58. Letter from Clare Street to Luciano Fabro, 12 May 1975. SNGMA Archive, GMA A37/2/105/16.
59. See https://www.carmignanodivino.it/it/2016/05/alberto-moretti-e-carmignano/?pdf=7721
60. Letter from Clare Street to Maria Gloria Bicocchi, dated 26 May 1975. SNGMA Archive, GMA A37/2/105/16.
61. SNGMA Archive, GMA A37/2/105/16.
62. Letter from Clare Street to Bill Viola, 17 July 1975. SNGMA Archive, GMA A37/2/105/15
63. Letter from Richard Demarco to Maria Gloria Bicocchi, 18 September 1975. SNGMA Archive, GMA A37/2/105/15
64. GMA A37/2/104 Box 104.
65. Programme of the trip available at SNGMA Archive, GMA A37/2/105/2.
66. "Form of Catalogue for the Edinburgh Festival Exhibition", Edinburgh Arts 1975.
67. SNGMA Archive, GMA A37/2/105/17. See also *To Callanish From Hagar Qim*, with an introduction of L. Lippard (Edinburgh: The Richard Demarco Gallery, 1975), page not numbered.
68. SNGMA Archive, GMA A37/2/105/17.
69. G. Sartorelli, *Punto di vista. Cronache e riflessioni attorno a un'esperienza artistica* (Venice 1998), pp. 26–27 (The Translation into English is by the author of this chapter).
70. I would like to thank the Remo Bianco Foundation for their help and support to investigate this work.
71. Rosalind Krauss, 'Grids', *October*, #9, 1979, pp. 50–64.
72. Angela Madesani, private communication, via email, 7 April 2021.
73. SNGMA Archive, GMA A37/2/105/16
74. *To Callanish From Hagar Qim*, with an introduction of L. Lippard (Edinburgh: The Richard Demarco Gallery, 1975), page not numbered.
75. *A journey From Hagar Qim to The Ring of Brodgar*, edited by D. Bellman (Edinburgh: The Richard Demarco Gallery, 1976), p. 1.

3

Musings / an afternoon with Richard Demarco and Terry Ann Newman

Elaine Shemilt and Stephen Partridge

In August 2020, four of us sat together over lunch in the village of Howgate near Penicuik. At the age of ninety Richard Demarco was relaxed and reflective as the Scottish summer drew to a lazy end, swans foraged in the pond in front of the cottage, and we could see the Pentland Hills in the distance.

Privileged to have been Richard's friends for so many years and to have witnessed first -hand or indeed been a part of so many of the extraordinary adventures that he had initiated over his long life-time, we might have expected that the enfant terrible, this elder statesman of British Art might have slowed down. Not a bit of it. His mind was irresistibly energetic, engulfing artists, philosophers and thinkers into a swirling focus of activity and passion.

Richard Demarco has been an artist, gallery director, an educator, a promoter of theatre and is a cultural commentator and notably has been a key figure in the European avant-garde both in Scotland and internationally since the 1960s. He writes prolifically and eloquently, although his documentation is more often found in magazines and articles as the result of conversations and chance collisions.

He is a European hungering after classical cultural extremes sometimes confusing the heretic and mystic– a legend in his own time. His art extends to a recognition of other artists who have the

Figure 1: Richard Demarco in Howgate, August 2020. [Image courtesy of Elaine Shemilt.]

Figure 2: Richard Demarco with Elaine Shemilt's sculptures at Traquair House, Peeblesshire, Scotland. [Image courtesy of Elaine Shemilt.]

research into the valuable resource that can be found within the Richard Demarco Archive. The following chapter is the result of our discussion.

Richard is a Scottish Italian with Irish heritage. In keeping with the recognition that his 18th century Demarco ancestors were farmers and shepherds from Picinisco and that his maternal ancestors were farmers in the Tuscan mountains around the city of Bargo, Richard has little time for the politeness of either the English or Scottish artworld, more often than not refuting both.

This gap in the historical canon of knowledge is slightly puzzling because within the Richard Demarco archives – a portion of which is at the Scottish National Gallery of Modern Art, (representing activities from 1963 to 1995) and a portion at the Demarco European Foundation (at Summerhall in Edinburgh) – there are many traces of exchanges between Italy and Scotland promoted by Demarco as part of his larger European network and contribution to the Edinburgh Festival. These documents include photographs, ephemera, notes, catalogues and artworks that feature events involving relevant Italian or Italian-based artists, producers, performers, directors, critics including: Palma Bucarelli, the Count Panza di Biumo, Giulio Paolini, Jannis Kounellis, Bruno Ceccobelli, Toti Scialoja, Carlo Quartucci and Carla Tatò, Mimmo Rotella, Mario Merz, Fabrizio Plessi, Achille Bonito Oliva, Maria Gloria Conti Bicocchi, Giuseppe Chiari, and Guido Sartorelli.

Richard began his career as a teacher and explorer of the avant-garde across Europe. In the face of early prejudice and ongoing difficulties he has always remained loyal to Edinburgh and Scotland, but in reality, has spent a lifetime as both an Italian and a Scot.

capacity to make us aware of the irrationality of our normality. Many of these artists are now famously celebrated but when Richard Demarco introduced them to centre-stage they were often unknown and their work was perceived to be difficult, challenging and unconformist.

Although much research and many publications have been devoted to Demarco's endeavours,[1] by comparison relatively little is written about his exchanges with Italy, how he promoted Italian visual and performing arts in Scotland and how he influenced the Italian cultural context. The network built by Demarco around his Italian connections has only been partially identified and is consequently under-acknowledged. By gaining the Italian perspective into Richard Demarco as a major thinker and visionary, we can hopefully provide the catalyst for further documentation and

Anyone who knows Richard or has heard him speak will be aware of his ability to weave history into the present and vice a versa. Listening to Richard speak requires an alert mind to keep abreast of his brilliant, freewheeling thought associations, refreshingly punctuated with his undiminished humour, but his message is serious. It comes from a deep desire to forge a cohesive cultural identity between people who have a common artistic heritage.

In 1970 Richard Demarco wrote:

"I had always wanted an exhibition which would restore my faith in the activity of the visual art in 20th Century society, and which would help redefine the role of the gallery Director. I had looked for an exhibition which would emphasize the artist's role as a powerful defender of the truth inherent in fairy tales and as a magician be able to revive our sense of wonder. I wanted an exhibition which would free the artist if he wished from the responsibility of making master works, revealing more clearly his act of creating and his acceptance of his role as a performer involving every new means of communication with the 'so called' layman. I wanted an exhibition which would weaken the spirit of materialism, from which more than ever the artist must rescue us."[2]

To understand the nature of Richard Demarco's understanding of what it is to be an Italo-Scot or indeed to be a European, it is necessary to understand that Richard Demarco shares the philosophy of his friend the late Joseph Beuys – "the capital of the world is not the money as we understand it, but the capital is the human ability for creativity, freedom and self-determination in all their working places."[3]

In our conversation with Demarco where we were discussing his childhood and what led to his extraordinary career, we were not surprised when the subject rapidly broadened Richard told us that in

the mid-first century – with the expansion of the Roman Empire and migrating Germanic tribes – Celtic culture and Insular Celtic languages had become restricted.

"I happen to believe that the 20th Century art world feeds on itself, and artists see the map of Europe in a distorted way – hence the gathering of artists at the Basel Art fair and the Cologne Kunstmarkt, rather than gathering at holier places where, perhaps, in the past, the wisest men went on pilgrimages. I speak not only of the great medieval University centres and the Holy Islands of Iona and Torcello, but also of Stonehenge. We must go further back than the Renaissance spirit to find a significant way to develop so called artistic concepts, knowing of course that there is no progress in art, merely discovery."

However, in 2020 as Richard Demarco celebrated his 90th birthday it was important to note that 2020 was also the 80th anniversary of a tragic event which coloured the life of Richard Demarco as a small boy in Scotland.

On July 2nd in 1940, Italy declared war against the Allies. This caused mob violence in parts of Edinburgh including Portobello, making it impossible for Richard to attend his St John's Roman Catholic Primary School. Italy's entry into the war devastated the community of Italo-Scots largely due to Winston Churchill's famous order to "Collar the Lot". As Richard recalled:

This caused every member of the Anglo-Italian communities throughout the British Isles who had any connection with Mussolini's Fascist regime to be interned, and that included those that were to be shipped to internment camps in Canada and Australia. Tragically, the cruise liner Arandora Star was carrying many Scottish Italians when it was torpedoed with great loss of life, including the father and uncle of the artist Eduardo Paolozzi. He was fortunate that he was not on board; however, he was imprisoned in Edinburgh aged 16. I do not think that particular generation of Italo-Scots ever recovered. However, I experienced the world of the Italo-Scottish community on the coast of the River Clyde when I was evacuated to Largs. There I first discovered the spirit of modernism in the architecture of two buildings owned by two Italian families, the Nardini and the Castelvecchi families. My father was appointed manager of the Castelvecchi family's magnificent, three storey high building known as "The Moorings". Both the Moorings and the Nardini's café brought the full glory of pre-war Italian culture to Glaswegian holiday makers and gave me good reason to think that, when the war was over, I could experience the Art Deco architecture of Italy for myself. I arrived in Largs in time to experience the devastating Clyde-side air raid suffered by the citizens of Greenock and Gourock. It should also be noted that, as a result of the air raid on Portobello, I made a point of attending the funeral of two young Luftwaffe airmen who died on that ill-fated air raid. As an altar server and member of St John's Church choir, I also became conscious of the presence of Italian prisoners of war attending Sunday Mass.

Precisely 804 mostly Italian and German internees and prisoners of war lost their lives when the Canada bound transport ship The Arandora Star they were sailing in was sunk by a German U boat. A quarter of the Scottish Italians who lost their lives were from Edinburgh. To understand Richard Demarco, it is necessary to understand the profound depth of misery and despair that this event disproportionally caused the Italian community in Edinburgh.

Richard says that he will never forget that day in Edinburgh when the bereaved Italians whose loved ones had been interned at Saughton were lost forever. The event was not adequately reported or acknowledged at the time and for many years was simply an event that British history pushed aside to be semi-forgotten. Whether this was out of a sense of guilt over the sloppy management of the

situation in the first place – many who were lost on that ship were simply aboard because they were Italian – or because this was a chapter in history that was still too raw and emotionally confusing amongst so much else during to dwell upon during the war. It is only in recent years that this tragedy has been investigated, reported upon and given more attention.

The effect on Richard as a young boy is palpable. Both parents were the children of Italian immigrants. They had a French-style café in Portobello and Richard fondly recalls the smell of coffee and cigar smoke. Outside the family home and warmth of the trattoria however, the atmosphere of mistrust, the prejudice and misunderstanding had a profound effect upon his outlook as a boy. He recalls that at the age of five, his father issued a stark warning to the family. "This will not be good for us" as Mussolini invaded Abyssinia. When Richard was aged nine, playing on Portobello beach, he clearly remembers running for his life as the bullets from spitfires tore into a damaged Junkers bomber and rained down on to the beach. Only 100 feet above him, Richard could see the stricken faces of the young German pilot before their air raid and their lives ended as they crashed into the Lammermuir hills.

Unlike his fellow artist Sir Eduardo Paolozzi, who suffered the loss of his father and his uncle on the Arandora Star, Richard did not leave Scotland when the opportunity arose. Like Eduardo, who was six years his senior, Richard attended the Holy Cross Academy. He says that his schoolteacher recognised that he too was destined for an artistic future and so he was given the desk that had previously been Eduardo Paolozzi's. Like his predecessor, Demarco went straight from School to Edinburgh College of Art, but in contrast to Paolozzi, Demarco began a life that both justified his decision to remain in Scotland and simultaneously galvanised him into thinking beyond the confines of Scotland as a nation. In 1947 Richard Demarco was quite overwhelmed by the first Edinburgh Festival. The impact of the sounds of the Vienna Philharmonic Orchestra, the German Lieder singing of Kathleen Ferrier and the French language production by the Louis Jouvet Company of Moliere's L'Ecole des Femmes. Richard made his leap of faith. The Lord Provost said at the time "This is the flowering of the Human Spirit, the process of healing after the pain of War". Profound words, which Richard Demarco acted upon and never lost sight of. Richard refers to the Edinburgh Festival as "his University."

For the Catholic community, 1950 was defined as 'The 1950 Holy Year'. Richard accompanied his father to Rome on a Pilgrimage. As he recalled:

We travelled through France to the border at Ventimiglia, and the Italian Riviera to find ourselves in the Eternal City of Rome. On seeing Central Station in Rome, I could not help but compare it to Edinburgh's Waverley Station because it was a manifestation of modern architecture in white marble. My experience of attending St Peter's and the High Mass introduced me to the genius of Michelangelo's Pieta and Bernini's High Altar.

After leaving art school in 1953 and military service, in 1957 Richard became the art master at Dun Scotus Academy in Edinburgh for ten years. During 1963 he became involved with Jim Haynes in co-founding the Traverse Theatre Club (15 James Court, Lawnmarket, Edinburgh) a former dosshouse and brothel also known as Kelly's Paradise and Hell's Kitchen. The club's activities gave him close contact with the avant-garde; a theatre conference was organised by

Jim Haynes, John Calder and Kenneth Tynan and included a happening involving American artist Allan Kaprow. At the outset Demarco set up a small exhibition space for visual art but this was too small for his ambitions and in 1966 he and his associates left the Traverse to establish what became the Richard Demarco Gallery. These early years laid the foundation for a career that provided a lifeline for many young pioneers of the avant-garde whom Scotland and the world have since recognised as great artists.

In 1967, Richard was appointed director of the Edinburgh International Festival programmes of contemporary art which he held up to and including the Festival of 1991 (when Brian McMaster, the incoming Director, did not want visual art in his programmes).

By 1970 many gallery directors were heading to New York. It was an exciting time, fast and furious. Fortunate artists were experiencing measures of liberation and the possibility of serious money, gallerists and curators were cashing in. Despite the opportunity and invitations, Richard turned his back on the crowd and headed for eastern Europe to explore the Contemporary Art worlds of Poland and Romania behind the Iron Curtain. It was not and has never been an easy career move.

In 1968, Richard travelled for the first time to Poland and then from Warsaw flew to Bucharest for his visit to Romania. Having ventured forth into Europe into what would have then been considered as the wrong side of the Iron Curtain, Richard Demarco brought difficult, vulnerable, controversial artists out of their environments and put them into the limelight at the Edinburgh festival. Simultaneously, Richard Demarco's approach distinguished these artists, writers and musicians from the culture of their surrounding politics just enough to give them sufficient oxygen to breathe and develop.

His new gallery in Edinburgh's Melville Crescent, New Town, had the ambitious aim of internationalising the Scottish contemporary art scene, a task he has pursued relentlessly for forty years. In 1974, the Melville Crescent premises were sold and then Richard moved to Great King Street. Then in 1975 it moved to the Historic Royal Mile, to a building known as Monteith House, neatly wedged between Carruber's Close and John Knox's House. Here it remained for a decade until circumstances in the early 80s left the Scottish Arts to cease their grants. The Gallery now became totally dependent on help from its 'Friends' to support it through these hard times. With the help of 750 Friends of the Arts and the Arts Council, £40,000 was eventually found. The Gallery moved to No. 10 Jeffrey Street, just around the corner which property was rented from the Council. It remained her for six years from 1982 to 1987 when by a most generous decision of Edinburgh District Council the Gallery was given the right to buy a splendid four storey building in Blackfriars Street for a nominal amount of £10,000. With the restoration of this building Richard was able to concentrate once again on his theatre programme and it hosted over the year many memorable productions. These productions were to host many Italian, Dutch, Polish and generally European artists whose performances went on to become famous, but every step of the way Richard has been beset by financial problems and constraints. In August 1980, the Scottish Arts Council had removed the Demarco Gallery's annual grant and the funding for his Festival programmes.

"The artists whom I dealt with were not making art to be sold. In Eastern Europe their art could not be sold. I was dealing directly with artists who were making art that was pure of heart". Thus, Richard stoked the embers of what was to become another extraordinary enlightenment in Scotland. He began the job of introducing powerful and potent artists who offered new ways of seeing and thinking to Scotland. They were also writers, philosophers and pioneers of the avant-garde. Through the Edinburgh festival, Richard gave them a platform to show their work: the Polish artist Tadeusz Kantor from Cracow, whose Cricot 2 theatre company gave Scotland a first taste of European expressionist theatre; the abstract and photorealist painter Gerhard Richter from Dusseldorf, the Serbian artist Marina Abramović and many others, but the artist who most profoundly influenced Richard was a German artist called Joseph Beuys.

Until Beuys died in January of 1986, Beuys and Demarco shared an intense and enabling artistic and creative relationship. In many ways Beuys validated Richards indefatigable struggle to embody everything that he so passionately believed in.

They were kindred spirits with a shared passion, but what led to this deep understanding of the value of art between the two men? What led to this intense bond? One man had been in the Nazi youth, then as a fifteen-year-old had partaken in the Nuremberg rally and later volunteered for the Luftwaffe. The other, a man nine years his junior, was an Italian at heart, who as boy had been bullied in Edinburgh and had lost Italian compatriots in the Arandora tragedy in 1940. A shared Anthroposophical perspective of art and life may give some insight into this alliance.

Both Demarco and Beuys saw the possibility that art could transcend beyond the limitations of war. They had both survived a war and had each independently determined that the mark of a true artist is someone who experiences an essential need of life, just as someone experiences hunger and thirst. The art that both Beuys aspired to make and Demarco aspired to present, must pose certain questions on the nature of being human and what value our place as humans is within the Universe.

> The art of Joseph Beuys provided a source of inspiration to an art world which must take seriously what Beuys defined as *La Difesa della Natura* with particular reference to his respect for the cultural heritage of Italy.[4]

In Howgate, Penicuik on that day in August the sun was by now hanging low in the sky and there was the usual Scottish chill of late afternoon in the air. Suddenly the spirited and agile 90-year-old was on his feet. Arms flung-wide, Richard emphatically reminded us that this year 2020 was also the 700th anniversary of the Declaration of Arbroath. This declaration (according to Richard) was an appeal to the people of Rome asking to be recognised in Europe.

> On the European front, by 1320 Scottish relations with the papacy were in crisis after the Scots defied papal efforts to establish a truce with England. When the pope excommunicated Robert I and three of his barons, the Scots sent the Declaration of Arbroath as part of a diplomatic counter-offensive. The pope wrote to Edward II urging him to make peace, but it was not until 1328 that Scotland's independence was acknowledged.

Laughingly we remarked upon Richard's interesting perspective. In current political climes it is a controversial subject, but for our purposes at least, this historical and political fine line between Rome and Scotland provides yet another justification for Richard's desire to recognise connecting philosophical concepts in the spirit of a renaissance rather than dwell on political barriers that prevent artistic progress.

By way of an example, the 1976 Edinburgh Arts journey from Hagar Quim in Malta to the Ring of Brodgar in Orkney drew on the world of artists such as Paul Neagu, Joseph Beuys, Mario Merz, John David Mooney and Tadeusz Kantor.

As Richard said:

> focusing the cultural and historical links which bound the Mediterranean culture and that of Malta, Sardinia and the Italian mainland with that of the former Yugoslavia, Romanised France and the all- embracing Celtic culture which identified the British Isles geographically and historically within the continent of Europe, it therefore explored the history of the culture of the Italo-Scot , which defined me as a citizen of Europe originating in a Romano-Celtico European world from the shorelines of the Mediterranean to those of the British Isles.

Starting with only the traces of exchanges between Italy and Scotland as promoted by Demarco within his larger European network, we came to understand that within the Richard Demarco Archives there are many references to the Scottish artists who were enabled by Richard's cultural exchanges with Italy. Why has this not been researched into more fully? It is because Richard considered that Italian artists had no particular need of his intervention in the 1960's, 1970's and 1980's? Scotland on the other hand, needed the Italian influence and culture. With a few exceptions, it was a drab and restricted artworld, largely dominated by the Royal Scottish Academy with a limited vision, led by a hierarchy of men and the heavy hand of provincial patriotism. Richard was keenly aware of these limitations in Scotland. After his first trip to his father's home country, he describes the sensation and thrill of stepping out of the train into stations in Paris and Rome, the fantastic architecture, the smart and elegantly dressed people, the food, the wine and the coffee, not to mention the design and artistic vision.

In 2020 there were celebratory articles in the Scottish press – lauding Scotland's first real presence at the Venice Biennale in 1990.[5] The Biennale director Giovanni Carandente wrote that he considered the Scottish show 'one among the most important events of the 44th International exhibition of art'. The organisers of the 1990 exhibition acknowledged Demarco as the inspiration for their show following his assertion in 1988 that it was high time that Scotland "should claim its place at the art world's biggest table".[6] However, this rather ignored Demarco's five decades of interaction and activity with, and within the western world's most famous bi-annual exhibition in *La Serenissima*.

It is important to understand that Richard Demarco's connection with Italy is a constituent part of his 'journeys'. *The Road to Meikle Seggie*[7] is not a mythological or allegorical journey but a five-decade- long series of real physical journeys across and between the countries of Europe. They could also be said to have been pre-ceded by the early trips the teenager, Richard undertook with his father to Paris, Rome and his ancestors' villages in the southern province of Lazio, when his mind was opened to the idea of Europe as a cultural landscape. As an adult, starting in the late 1960s Richard undertook journeys of discovery to Poland, Yugoslavia, Italy, Romania, Ireland, France, Malta, Sardinia, West Germany (GDR), Corsica, Corfu, Greece, Cycladean Islands, Channel Islands, Netherlands, Bosnia, Croatia, Hungary, Czech Republic, Serbia, Bulgaria, Lithuania, Georgia. These early journeys were conceived as a mobile Summer School

entitled Edinburgh Arts, but quickly developed into an important thread of what Demarco calls his Gesamtkunstwerk – a total artwork. Lucy Lippard, the American writer and critic noted in 1983:

> The person who has done most to conceptualize the connection between such contemporary lines on the land, ritual art and the ancient notion of the journey, is Richard Demarco a Scottish artist turned arts administrator/organizer/spiritual tour guide. An indefatigable traveller and proselytiser who cares deeply about the soul of contemporary culture, Demarco began his 'Edinburgh Arts Journey' in 1976, though he had been sowing ideas about ancient/ modern connections for several years before that. The annual voyage with artists, students and interested participants explores sites in Sardinia, Malta, France, Italy, Spain, Portugal, the Azores, and the British Isles, and is itself Demarco's work of art about these connections.[8]

Richard Demarco's first substantive foray with Italian art was in March 1967 with *Contemporary Italian Art works by 37 artists*, which included Enrico Baj, Alberto Burri, Giuseppe Capogrossi, Pietro Consagra, Lucio Del Pezzo, Jannis Kounellis, Piero Manzoni, Pino Pascali, and Salvatore Scarpitta. This show constituted a major coup at the time for its non-cosmopolitan setting at the Richard Demarco Gallery, Melville Street, in Edinburgh in only its second year of operation.

The following year (1968) Demarco made his first visit to the Venice Biennale, which he has visited every time since. It was remarkable for organisational problems, threats of a student sit-in of the Accademia di Belle Arti and many artists involved in the "boycott the Biennale movement".[9]

During this period and one of the seminal events in Demarco's career was the 1970 *Strategy: Get Arts* exhibition (the title is a palindrome) held in Edinburgh

College of Art. The event jolted the conservative Edinburgh art establishment from its *belle-peinture* slumber – 40 Dusseldorf-based avant-garde artists took over the college and three weeks of mayhem ensued, much of it chronicled by Demarco and the Glasgow photographer George Oliver.

Demarco's next substantial Italian show was during Edinburgh Arts in 1974 (August/September), at his 18a Great King Street Galery, entitled *7 Galleria del Cavallino Artists*. The exhibition included Anselmo Legnagni, Miroslav Sutej, Paolo Patelli, Giancarlo Teardo. A mixture of Italian and Croatian artists the exhibition was the first of many collaborations with Paolo and Gabriella Cardazzo co-directors of the Cavallino Gallery in Venice.

The most comprehensive Venice exhibition undertaken by Demarco came in 2019 where many aspects of The Demarco Archive were able to be presented in a huge salon of La Scuola Grande di San Marco, Campo San Zanipolo (6th to 14th May 2021). Under the title of 'Art and Healing' the exhibition also included a wide-ranging symposium bringing together many strands and themes of the archive and Richard's activities over the past seven decades in grand surroundings. The Symposium and Comversatie included Sonia Rolak, Dr. Radu Varia, Giuseppe Meroni, Dr. Giuliano Gori, Miranda McPhail, Nicola Beckett (representing Monsignor Patrick Burke), Andrew Marr, Francesco da Mosto, Dr. Deirdre MacKenna, Sam Smith representing Alan Smith, Dr. Oliver Bray, Sheila Colvin, Faynia Williams, Richard Crane, Professor Stephen Partridge, Professor Elaine Shemilt, Alberta Tominato, Gabriella Cardazzo, Professor Bill Beech, Dr. Anthony Schrag, Michele Ciacciofera, Renato Qualia, Caroline Wiseman, Amanda Catto, Professor Sarah Wilson and Dr. Klara Kemp Welch

and a programme of film and with films by Margaret Tait, Gabriella Cardazzo, Paolo Cardazzo, Wendy and Devora Cutler, Elaine Shemilt, Michael Lloyd, Marco Federici, and Pippa Bellasis. In the programme notes Demarco stated:

> I regard the Demarco Archive as possibly the first example of an art-work in the state of incompletion, expressing the values and aspirations of the first-ever Edinburgh Festival. It is essentially a unique academic resource, identifying a war-torn Europe giving birth to a festival of all the arts, the Archive (as exhibited here) ascends to the condition of a large-scale artwork and thus can be best described by the German word "Gesamtkunstwerk" (a total artwork). It expresses Joseph Beuys' concept of *social sculpture.....* it juxtaposed the art of Ian Hamilton-Finlay, Paul Neagu, Joseph Beuys, Tadeusz Kantor – with that of the senior art students and teachers at Glenalmond College. "Art and Healing" as an exhibition and symposium, was planned to strengthen the cultural dialogue between Scotland and Europe with a particular emphasis on Romanian, Italian, Polish, German and French cultural aspects of Edinburgh Arts programmes since 1973.

One of the purposes in writing this chapter was to gain a perspective into Richard Demarco's vision as a major thinker and visionary. He introduced artists from Scotland to Italy and in turn promoted Italian visual art in Scotland and this cultural exchange was something that both Richard Demarco and Joseph Beuys profoundly believed in.

Although not prolific, the late James Howie was an important artist who exemplifies how Richard Demarco influenced the cultural context.

James Howie was a Scottish artist from Dundee on the East Coast of Scotland. He loved the international spirit of the Demarco Gallery and collaborated most effectively with his fellow Edinburgh Arts participants, particularly Joan Hughson, Alice Beberman and Norman Mommens who, as a Belgian sculptor, established himself in the heartland of Puglia in the world of the Masseria Spigolizzi near Lecce. Howie assimilated into this particular unique Apulian world. He thrived and benefited from being introduced to the entourage of Richard Demarco's friends and acquaintances. John Hale, the English sculptor then domiciled in Como became a particular friend and introduced Jim to the Milanese art world.

In the world of Count Giuseppe Panza di Biumo in his great collection under the roof of his home, the Renaissance Villa Litta on a hilltop in the centre of Varese, Richard has a distinct memory of Jim Howie enjoying a dinner where Edinburgh Arts artists were the guests of Count Panza and his wife, Contessa 'Bupa' Panza. On that particular occasion, Douglas Hall and his wife Matilda were also enjoying Count Panza's hospitality. If the Panza Collection had found a home in Scotland (as was Count Panza's intention), Richard also have introduced Scotland to the work of the leading international avant-garde artists, such as Sol LeWitt, Bruce Nauman, James Turrell, and Italian artists. Through no lack of vision or enthusiasm unfortunately not all of Richard's plans came to fruition. Richard introduced artists such as Howie to the Italian galleries connected to the world of the Cavallino, particularly the Valsecchi and art/tapes/22, the latter was a leading gallery, promulgating the importance of video arts.

Back in Scotland in the world of Edinburgh Arts, Howie encountered artists of the calibre of the Chicago-based artist John David Mooney. Howie personified that spirit of internationalism and risk-taking "I wished in the seventies to associate with the art world of Scotland. "Howie introduced Richard Demarco to the Brown and White Caterthuns, the prehistoric hill forts which he considered as manifestations of mankind's harmonious relationship with nature. For Howie they were expressions of what he considered as 'land art'. Through Richard Demarco, Howie came to play a prominent part in the 1976 Edinburgh Arts programme linking Italy with Scotland, particularly in Sardinia and Puglia and the friendship with Gabriella and the Cavallino Gallery.

The year 2020 marked the 100th anniversary of the birth of Joseph Beuys and this must be acknowledged because the spirit of Beuys, the philosophy and understanding that Richard Demarco and Joseph Beuys shared permeates everything. Joseph Beuys saw in Jim Howie the spirit of a true avant-gardist.

Howie comments: 'Nature is the source of everything I do. The force of Nature. The power of Nature. In Scotland there is more evidence of Nature – openness, purity of light, the continuing presence of sea and sky'.[10] During his long and productive life, this simple philosophy is at the heart of much of what Richard Demarco has managed to achieve.

Elsewhere in this book about Richard Demarco's Italian influences the authors have mentioned or written about 'the Road to Meikle Seggie'. A small point that came across during the conversation with Richard on that August afternoon has continued to resonate and begins to complete an important picture.

In one of Richard's articles entitled 'Pastorizia' he explains why he must take seriously the fact that his Italian ancestors were farmers and shepherds. It gives a new meaning to his continuing need to explore 'the Road to Meikle Seggie', which is basically the road to a hill farm on the lower slopes of the Ochil Hills.

This profound and philosophical

THE DEMARCO EUROPEAN ART FOUNDATION
A Registered Scottish Charity No. SCO. 18584

Director: Professor Richard Demarco
O.B.E., Hon. R.S.A., R.S.W., Hon. F.R.I.A.S., Hon. LL.D (Dundee), Hon. D.F.A (Atlanta)
Deputy Director: Terry Ann Newman
Archivist: Steve Robb
Building Two, New Parliament House, 5 Regent Road, Edinburgh EH7 5BL
Tel: 00 44 (0) 131 5570707 Fax: 00 44 (0) 131 5575972

THE DEMARCO EUROPEAN ART FOUNDATION
At
THE VENICE BIENNALE 2003
At
THE CENTRO NAUTICO, GIUDECCA

An Exhibition and Symposium
Presenting
LIMITED EDITION GICLEE PRINTS
Each signed and dated
Defining the 4 aspects of
THE DEMARCO PHOTOGRAPHIC ARCHIVES
Relating to the sections
Devoted to
JOSEPH BEUYS, IAN HAMILTON FINLAY and TADEUSZ KANTOR

As well as the section devoted to the GERMAN ART
at the EDINBURGH FESTIVALS 1970 (Strategy: Get Arts)
1980- 10th Anniversary of "Strategy: Get Arts"
1980-Joseph Beuys "What's Up For 1984"
1982-Treffpunkt Parnass in collaboration with Goethe Institut London
1983-Joseph Beuys 12 Hour Lecture
1990-Gunther Uecker "Pictlandish Garden"
1995-25th Anniversary- Strategy:Get Arts
1995- Celebrating 25th Anniversary of Celtic Kinloch Rannoch-The Scottish
Symphony –
Henning Christiansen and Ursula Reuter

An exhibition of art works by
ALAN DAVIE, IAN HAMILTON FINLAY
AND
GUNTHER UECKER
Celebrating the cultural dialogue between Scotland and Germany

A FIVE-DAY SYMPOSIUM FROM
7th –12th June 2003
considering, among other topics, the relationship between the Venice Biennale,
the Documenta and the Edinburgh Festival and the influence of Goethe and
Ruskin upon the cultural heritage of Scotland, Germany and Italy.

Figure 3: A 2003 publicity notice illustrating the often complex activities undertaken by Demarco.

connection to those who work in the fields is the link which not least combines religion, symbolism, aspects of architecture, aesthetics and art.

Farming and landscape played an important part in the post – World War Two history of Joseph Beuys. Over a period of three years, he farmed with his friends the Van der Grinten brothers. This experience of farming helped in his period of recovery from the serious physical and mental war wounds that he had suffered. This prepared Beuys for his role as an artist- environmentalist and as the co-founder of the German Green party.

Much later and as a result of his collaboration with Richard, Joseph Beuys was inspired by his concern for the destructive forces caused by earthquakes in Italy.This led to the patronage he received from the Count Bubi Durini and his wife Lucrezia di Domizio. Richard also benefitted from his collaborations in Scilly with the artist Andrea Cusumano who, for a while, was Deputy Mayor of Culture for the City of Palermo, and his friend Michele Cacciofera, who is a key figure in the definition of the Italian dimension in Mediterranean culture.

This enabling 16-year relationship that these two men sustained until the death of Joseph Beuys cannot be underestimated. Beuys also played a part in Richard Demarco's exchanges with Italy, how he promoted Italian visual and performing arts in Scotland and how he influenced the Italian cultural context.

The ideas generated by these two men together influenced the network built by Demarco around his Italian connections and much of these ideas can be sourced back to a type of anthroposophical and intellectually comprehensible – almost spiritual view of the world. As Richard acknowledges, we must go further back than a Renaissance spirit to find a significant way to develop so called artistic concepts, in the full knowledge of course that there is no progress in art – there is merely discovery.

Joseph Beuys concluded in his discussion with Richard Demarco in 1982 about the planting of 7,000 trees:

Love is the most creative and matter-transforming power. You see in this context it is very simply expressed. Now it is not shown in very interesting diagrams which one could also bring to this discussion … But to promote this interest for all these necessities to the real anthropology and not his fashionable way of speaking about anthropology … in this relationship I start with the most simple-looking activity, but it is a most powerful activity; it is planting trees.

Endnotes

1. These include the exhibition at the Royal Scottish Academy of Art and Architecture (27 November 2010 – 9 January 2011) and the book E. McArthur & A. Watson (Eds.), *10 Dialogues. Richard Demarco Scotland and the European Avant Garde* (Edinburgh: Royal Scottish Academy of Art and Architecture, 2010).
2. *International magazine of the Arts*, Winter 1970, n. 2.
3. 'Art into Time, interview with Joseph Beuys', *Artforum*, 1969, p. 47.
4. Richard Demarco's Newsletter – 22 February 2021.
5. C.f.: Susan Mansfield, 1990: *When three Scottish sculptors took over the Venice Biennale*, , The Scotsman, Saturday, 27th June 2020.
6. *Ibidem*.
7. 'To travel the road to Meikle Seggie is to undertake any journey which offers unexpected opportunities for intellectual growth and self-discovery'. From the back-cover text of the book, Richard Demarco, *The Road to Meikle Seggie* (Edinburgh: Luath Press Ltd 2015).
8. Lucy R. Lippard, *Overlay: Contemporary Art and the Art of Prehistory* (New York: Pantheon Book, 1983), p. 132.
9. Chiara Di Stefano, 'The 1968 Biennale. Boycotting the exhibition: An account of three extraordinary days', in C. Ricci (ed.), *Starting From Venice* (Milan: EtAl, 2010), pp. 10-133. Available at https://www.academia.edu/5708781/The_1968_Biennale_Boycotting_the_exhibition_An_acco unt_of_three_extraordinary_days (retrieved 5 April 2021).
10. McManus Museum and Art Gallery Guide, page 12. https://www.mcmanus.co.uk/sites/default/files/centurygallery.pdf - retrieved 5 April 2021.

4

The International Reach of Mara Coccia: the *Roma Punto Uno* Exhibition

Francesca Gallo

Richard Demarco performed an important role in promoting knowledge of contemporary Italian culture in Scotland: only a year after opening, the Richard Demarco Gallery held the exhibition *Contemporary Italian Art* in collaboration with Galleria Nazionale d'Arte Moderna di Roma (GNAM), the main Italian institution dedicated to contemporary art.[1] This exposition was the Scottish version of *L'Art Actuel en Italie. Aspetti dell'arte italiana contemporanea (Aspects of Italian Contemporary Art)*, an exhibition promoted by the Ente Nazionale Industrie Turistiche (National Body for Tourism Industries) in the context of the *Semaines italiennes* in Cannes, on the occasion of the 9th Museums Week (19 December 1965 – 2 January 1966). Placed in the Municipal Casino by Giorgio De Marchis, more than sixty artworks were displayed again in Spring 1966 at GNAM.[2] Among these, the *Natale di Roma* (1964, Figure 1) by Franco Angeli, that was shown in the following Spring 1967 at the Richard Demarco Gallery. Angeli's *Natale di Roma* represents the renowned Capitoline wolf on a pedestal with an inscription from a fragment of emperor Augustus' *Index Rerum Gestarum*. The composition, entirely rendered in blue and golden hues, is covered by a dark veil that allows shapes and colours to shine through with difficulty: a stylistic and technical solution that alludes to the real or mnestic emergence of political symbols in a Rome in full economic boom, peppered with infrastructure building sites, with *dolce vita* in Via Veneto and an artistic *bohème* in Piazza del Popolo. Still owned by the artist, *Natale di Roma* was at the time in storage at GNAM at the request of Palma Bucarelli, who had seen it at the Angeli solo show at Studio d'Arte Arco d'Alibert, and who managed to purchase it for the museum collection only a few years later, in 1970.[3]

This quick digression evokes – albeit briefly – the historical depth of the figure and work of Mara Coccia, founder in December 1963 of Studio d'Arte Arco d'Alibert, a gallery that held an important role in the Roman art scene of the '60s for supporting emerging young artists such as Angeli, despite being less dominant than La Tartaruga, La Salita or L'Attico. The gallerist aimed to bring collectors of limited financial means closer to already historicized artists – such as Osvaldo Licini, Gastone Novelli, Antonio Sanfilippo, Gino Severini, Guido Strazza – through drawing, and to emerging figures, such as Eugenio Carmi, by whom she presents designs, multiples, and produces *Stripsody*, or Carlo Lorenzetti and Pasquale Santoro focusing, for example, on the artist jewel.[4] Moreover, in its first years of activity, the gallery stood out for the attention paid to the artist book and limited editions with original drawings, including genuine works of art such as *Frammenti capitolini* (1964) by Angeli, *Viaggio in Grecia* by Novelli, *Alfabeto* by Jannis Kounellis and Mario Diacono, as well as *Osvaldo Licini Cesare Vivaldi. Disegni e parole*, all published in 1966.

In 1968, the activity of Studio d'Arte Arco d'Alibert was also affected by a renewal of sculpture in an installation and procedural key, so much so as to promote a milestone experiment such as *Il percorso*: an exhibition in progress coinciding with the first Roman release of the Arte Povera group, and for which Giovanni Anselmo, Alighiero Boetti, Mario Merz, Aldo Mondino, Ugo Nespolo, Giulio Paolini, Gianni

Piacentino, Michelangelo Pistoletto and Gilberto Zorio set up the works in front to Mario Cresci's camera. The latter, goes beyond documenting to capture the fluid, playful and almost assembly atmosphere of the days: the works are composed and assembled as if in a long happening or workshop. Although the prospect of an ex post catalogue – such as the one that Plinio De Martiis was able to print shortly thereafter for *Teatro delle Mostre* – did not materialise, Cresci assembles the shots in eleven single copy compositions, in which he arranges the frames freely, without taking into account any sequence and therefore transforming the documentation into his own creative work, today in the collections of the Istituto Centrale per la Grafica (Central Institute for Graphics), thanks once again to the mediation of Mara Coccia.[5]

Figure 1: Franco Angeli, *Natale di Roma*, 1964. [On licence of Ministero della Cultura; Rome, Galleria Nazionale d'Arte Moderna e Contemporanea]

In 1970 the gallerist closed Studio d'Arte Arco d'Albert and – apart from a brief interlude in 1975–77 – returned to the capital in 1982 opening a new gallery, the Associazione Mara Coccia, named after herself, in tune with the new historical phase in which women, even in Italy, take a leading role in the art system. This strategic choice allows her to immediately mobilise the wealth of professional authority and relationships accumulated in the 1960s. Now her activity focused on exhibiting and promoting the collecting of historicised figures, which allowed her to open up to young artists as well, in particular those active in the field of sculpture and environmental installation. In this second season, she continued to pay attention to graphics with limited editions illustrated with original drawings that the artists made for their respective solo shows: between 1988 and 1992, for example, it was the turn of Claudio Verna, Giuseppe Uncini, Paolo Cotani, Mauro Staccioli and Achille Perilli, converging into the group exhibition *Cataloghi diseg-nati* (1997) together with original drawings by Alexander Calder (dating back to 1967), Emilio Scanavino and Giulio Turcato (1969), and by Piero Dorazio (1986), created for their respective solo shows.

Roma Punto Uno

In this new phase – thanks to the Italian Ministry of Foreign Affairs – the Associazione Mara Coccia conducted some international sorties, including the Scottish leg of *Roma Punto Uno,* hosted at the Richard Demarco Gallery in Edinburgh, from 7 February to 6 March 1989 (Figures 2a,b; 3). Coccia and Demarco did not know each other directly, but Alberto Di Mauro, director of the Italian Cultural

Figures 2a,b: Invite for the opening of the edition at Demarco Gallery in Edinburgh on 7 February. [On licence of Ministero della Cultura; Rome, Galleria Nazionale d'Arte Moderna e Contemporanea, Mara Coccia Fund.]

The Board of Directors of the Richard Demarco Gallery
and the Director of the Italian Institute for Scotland
have pleasure in inviting you to the opening of the exhibition

ROMA PUNTO UNO

WORKS BY 7Đ CONTEMPORARY ITALIAN ARTISTS

by

HIS EXCELLENCY THE ITALIAN AMBASSADOR
BORIS BIANCHERI

on

Tuesday 7th February 1989 at 7.00 p.m.

at

The Richard Demarco Gallery, 17-21 Blackfriars Street, Edinburgh EH1 1NB
Exhibition continues until 4th March, Mon.-Sat. 10.30-6.00 p.m.
The exhibition is presented with financial support from

Phaidon Press Ltd.

Scottish **A** rts Council   Edinburgh District Council
and the following representatives of the Italian Business Community in Scotland

ALFA ROMEO   **FIAT** *in Edinburgh*   **LANCIA** *in Edinburgh*
Fisher's Garage Edinburgh Ltd.   Hamilton Bros. Ltd.   Murray Motor Company

VALVONA & CROLLA
Italian Food and Wine Merchants

R.S.V.P. *The Secretary, The Italian Institute, 82 Nicolson Street, Edinburgh. Tel. (031) 668 2232*

THE RICHARD DEMARCO GALLERY in collaboration with the ITALIAN INSTITUTE
presents from the
GALLERIA MARA COCCIA IN ROME

Carla Accardi
Franco Angeli
Gianni Asdrubali
Ubaldo Bartolini
Luigi Boille
Paolo Buggiani
Antonio Capaccio
Tommaso Cascella
Bruno Ceccobelli
Mario Ceroli
Nino Corpora
Paolo Cotani
Claudio De Paolis
Gianni Dessi
Stefano Di Stasio
Piero Dorazio
Fabrizio Fabbri
Giosetta Fioroni
Andrea Fogli
Mauro Fogli
Pietro Fortuna
Gallian
Paola Gandolfi
Claudio Givani
Valeria Gramiccia
Mimmo Grillo
Piero Guccione
Antonietta Lama
Felice Levini
Giancarlo Limoni
Sergio Lombardo
Carlo Lorenzetti
Enrico Luzzi
Renato Mambor
Graziani Marini

Titina Maselli
Fabio Mauri
Vittorio Messina
Sabina Mirri
Elisa Montessori
Giulia Napoleone
Nunzio
Luigi Ontani
Roberto Pace
Giorgio Pagano
Claudio Palmieri
Achille Perilli
Alfredo Pirri
Vettor Pisani
Piero Pizzi Cannella
Enrico Pulsoni
Remo Remotti
Paolo Ristonchi
Lucia Romualdi
Mariano Rossano
Mimmo Rotella
Francesco Ruggiano
Giuseppe Salvatori
Rocco Salvia
Sergio Sarra
Tori Scialoja
Nino Scordia
Guido Strazza
Cesare Tacchi
Marco Tirelli
Carmine Torrincasca
Giuseppe Uncini
Claudio Verna
Simona Weller
Luisa Zanibelli

70 CONTEMPORARY ITALIAN ARTISTS
8th FEB.-4th MARCH 1989 Mon.-Sat. 10.30-6.00 p.m.

THE RICHARD DEMARCO GALLERY
17-21 BLACKFRIARS STREET (OFF THE ROYAL MILE) EDINBURGH
Tel. (031) 557 0707

ITALIAN INSTITUTE

ALFA ROMEO
Fisher's Garage Edinburgh Ltd.
Tel. (031) 337 2700

FIAT in Edinburgh
Hamilton Bros. Ltd.
Tel. (031) 334 6248

LANCIA in Edinburgh
Murray Motor Company
Tel. (031) 442 2800

VALVONA & CROLLA
Edinburgh's Specialist Italian Food and Wine Merchants

Phaidon Press Ltd.

Scottish Arts Council

Edinburgh District Council

Figure 3: Poster of the exhibition taking place between 8 February and 4 March 1989. [On licence of Ministero della Cultura; Rome, Galleria Nazionale d'Arte Moderna e Contemporanea, Mara Coccia Fund.]

Figure 4: Invite and leaflet for the edition held from 11 March to 4 April 1989 at Peacock Artspace, Aberdeen (Scotland). [On licence of Ministero della Cultura; Rome, Galleria Nazionale d'Arte Moderna e Contemporanea, Mara Coccia Fund.]

Institute in Edinburgh, whose venue was probably not large enough to host the event, thought of the Demarco Gallery, a private space with a long tradition,

always available for Italian culture, so much so that in 1986 the founder was awarded the title of "knight of the order of merit of the Italian Republic", and with whom in 1988 the Italian Cultural Institute had collaborated for the exhibition on Mario Merz.[6]

The *Roma Punto Uno* exhibition opened at the end of 1987 in the Roman venue of the Associazione Mara Coccia – at the time still shared with La Nuova Pesa, in the prestigious rooms on Via del Corso overlooking Piazza del Popolo – and the following year it is set up at Studio Marconi in Milan,[7] in Bologna and in Gaeta. In 1989, thanks to the interest of Rodolfo Buonavita, Italian consul for Scotland and Northern Ireland, *Roma Punto Uno* began an international tour touching, after the Richard Demarco Gallery, the Peacock Artspace in Aberdeen (Figure 4), Orpheus Gallery in Belfast as well as the Business Design Centre in London. In 1990 the exhibition was hosted again in Scotland by the Rozelle House Gallery in Ayr, then it traveled to Sweden, the Netherlands and ended the trip in Narni on the following year.[8]

The exhibition was designed to travel easily: seventy artists from the Roman area were involved, for an initial total of about 180 works strictly small in size (18x24 cm) corresponding to the first point (*punto uno*) of standard canvas sizes. A solution that, in addition to reducing transport costs, was more easily accessible – once again – to small and medium-size collectors. The operation was however capable of attracting attention to Italian identity through the name of the capital in the title of the exhibition, as the Scottish press readily recorded. In fact, in *The Arts*, Alice Bain wrote that the event 'offers nuggets of golden Rome which, like artistic postcards, almost make you wish were there'.[9] While Clare Henry, a few days later in the columns of the same newspaper underlined that fourteen of the selected artists had participated in the latest editions of the Venice Biennale noted the timing of the initiative was parallel to the great exhibition on Italian art hosted at the Royal Academy of London.[10]

Leafing through the bilingual catalogue that Mara Coccia printed in Italy with a text by Massimo Carboni and an illustration for each artist,[11] – you will meet established figures such as Carla Accardi, Franco Angeli, Mario Ceroli, Piero Dorazio, Tano Festa, Giosetta Fioroni, Sergio Lombardo , Carlo Lorenzetti, Renato Mambor, Titina Maselli, Fabio Mauri, Luigi Ontani, Achille Perilli, Vettor Pisani, Mimmo Rotella, Mario Schifano, Toti Scialoja, Cesare Tacchi, Giuseppe Uncini, Claudio Verna, most of whom the gallery owner was familiar with from the time of the Arco d'Alibert. But *Roma Punto Uno* also gathered exponents of the so-called Scuola di San Lorenzo – namely Bruno Ceccobelli, Gianni Dessì, Giuseppe Gallo, Paola Gandolfi, Nunzio, Piero Pizzi Cannella, Marco Tirelli – Piero Guccione, Felice Levini, Alfredo Pirri and younger artists such as Andrea Fogli, Mauro Folci, Lucia Romualdi, Carmine Tornincasa. The exhibition, therefore, offered a well-articulated overview of the Roman art scene from the second post-war period to the present day on the basis of the successful definition of *scuole romane* (Roman schools) that critics had just extended from the 1930s to the San Lorenzo Group,[12] in tune with the re-evaluation of the regional roots and of the *genius loci*, already emerged in the critical readings of the *Transavanguardia* movement. At the same time, *Roma Punto Uno* attested to the wide and branching network of Italian acquaintances and collaborations that Coccia established or strengthened in the late 1980s.

The pieces are in line with the artistic production of each author at that time: from the abstract compositions of the founders of Forma 1, of Verna, Elisa Montessori and Giulia Napoleone; to the figuration of Luigi Bartolini, Gandolfi, Levini, Ontani and Pisani; passing through the almost childlike forms of the so-called Roman Pop and the simplified ones of the San Lorenzo Group and Beatrice Mirri; from the black and white of Gianni Asdrubali to that of Lombardo; up to the more material-based research of Vittorio Messina, Romualdi, Scialoja, Uncini, to recall but a few. Finally, it is interesting to note that sculptors – such as Ceroli, Folci, Lorenzetti, for example – had also been 'reduced' to the small format belonging to pictorial conventions – who therefore proposed works in the form of bas-reliefs. Lastly, in line with the spirit of the initiative, some proposed works on paper.

Although, in fact, they are artworks in every respect, in our eyes today they are valued above all as a whole: most of them date back to 1987, hence they are part of the selection since the first Roman show (Figures 5–6), others are instead from 1988, added in the second phase, specifically for the international tour that started, as we said, from the Richard Demarco Gallery.[13] The substantial chronological and format uniformity favoured a staging that ordinarily stretched out like a continuous ribbon about a meter high, running along the walls of the exhibition spaces.[14] Instead, in the ample and in some ways, monumental rooms of the new venue of Richard Demarco's gallery, (which had recently moved to 17–21 Blackfriars Street in a historic building that featured large trefoil windows and an ogival ceiling on the first floor), the choice was probably a rhythmic staging, in which the works of each artist were grouped on a single register,

Figures 5 and 6:
Roma Punto Uno,
Nuova
Pesa/Associazione
Mara Coccia,
1987.
[On licence of
Ministero della
Cultura; Rome,
Galleria Nazionale
d'Arte Moderna e
Contemporanea,
Mara Coccia Fund.]

occupying both levels of the gallery.[15] The arrangement – which almost followed alphabetical order – saw sixty pieces on the ground floor and the same number on the upper floor, showing a significant reduction when compared to the beginning.

European Sorties

Roma Punto Uno was included in the program of the Italian Cultural Institute in Scotland, on whose leaflet the works of Perilli and Ceroli are reproduced, while the work of Dorazio illustrates the cover of the program of the Italian participation at the XXII Belfast Festival at Queen's. The exhibition took place in a climate of enthusiasm for the new course of USSR politics and the European unification process that reached an important turning point with the signing of the Maastricht Treaty in 1992. New possibilities were glimpsed for the art market following the introduction of the free movement of capital.

Effectively, Mara Coccia had already been collaborating with the Italian Ministry of Foreign Affairs for a few years,

thanks to which she created the exhibition *Forma 1 1947–1987. Accardi, Attardi, Consagra, Dorazio, Guerrini, Maugeri, Perilli, Sanfilippo, Turcato*.[16] Conceived for the fortieth anniversary of the foundation of the Roman abstraction group, the exhibition was hosted in the Musée de Brou, in Bourg-en-Bresse and in the Galerie Municipale d'Art Contemporain in Saint-Priest, near Lyon, in the spring of 1987, while in the autumn of the same year Bernd Krimmel,[17] curated a similar exhibition in Darmstadt, again with the collaboration of the gallerist, who had dedicated the historic exhibition-document to Forma 1 in 1965, at the Studio d'Arte Arco d'Alibert.[18] Moreover, the French sortie suggested to Coccia to undertake, with Valeria Gramiccia, the production of a series of videotapes titled *Nello studio di... (In the studio of ...)* These interview-documentaries, dedicated to artists of Forma 1, were shot in their ateliers and focus on creative process, methods and tools, as well as creating an opportunity to summarize the stages of a long career for the benefit of the general public.[19] Moreover, the videotape dedicated to Mario Ceroli could be at the heart of the artist's participation in the touring exhibition just a year later, as until then the sculptor had no other collaboration with Coccia.

In conclusion, we note an occasional international expansion of Mara Coccia's activities, in whose agenda Italian artists prevail in all the galleries she directs. Nevertheless, if in the 1960s the Studio d'Arte Arco d'Alibert hosted Asger Jorn (1964) and Martin Bradley (1965),[20] Paul Wunderlich (1965), the significant solo show of Alexander Calder (1967) and, finally, Winfred Gaul (1969),[21] from the 1980s the presence of overseas artists was rare, with the exception of a few residents in the capital. On the other hand, only in 1992 the Associazione Mara Coccia participated in the Foire International d'Art Contemporain in Paris and enquired into the terms for exhibiting at ARCO in Madrid.

The international tour of *Rome Punto Uno*, therefore, was essentially unique in the history of the gallery up to that moment. However, the success of the event called for an even richer second version of *Roma Punto Uno* at the beginning of the 21st century, which traveled to Seoul, Tokyo and Moscow, and which, in light of the pivotal role played by the MAE, suggested that Coccia donates the entire collection to the Italian State.[22]

Endnotes

1. See L. Leuzzi, 'Edimburgo-Roma 1967, connessioni italo-scozzesi sulle tracce della mostra *Contemporary Italian Art* alla Richard Demarco Gallery', *Storia dell'arte*, 2019, n. 1–2, pp. 205–215.
2. See *Aspetti dell'arte italiana contemporanea*, exhibition catalogue (Rome, March–April 1966) (Rome, Istituto Grafico Tiberino, [1966]); Rome, La Galleria Nazionale (LGN), Bio-iconographic Archive, *Mostre ed eventi fuori sede*, u.a. 27.
3. See A. Rorro, in S. Pinto (ed.), *Galleria nazionale d'arte moderna. Le collezioni del XX secolo*, Electa, Milan 2005, n. 27.2; LGN, Fondi Storici, Mara Coccia, bundle 6, u.a. 11.
4. For an overview, see F. Gallo, *Mara Coccia's Galleries in Rome*, in F. Gallo (ed.), *Works and Archives. Mara Coccia*, exhibition catalogue (Rome, 18 June – 20 September 2020) (Cinisello Balsamo: Silvana, 2020), pp. 14–19; L. Cherubini, '*Intervista a Mara Coccia*', in M. Calvesi and R. Siligato (eds.), *Roma anni '60. Al di là della pittura*, exhibition catalogue (Rome, 20 December 1990 –15 February 1991) (Rome: Carte Segrete, 1992), pp. 329–331.
5. See M.F. Bonetti, *Il percorso di Mario Cresci allo Studio Arco d'Alibert, Roma, 22 marzo 1968. Origini, funzioni, significati di una sequenza fotografica, dall'archivio al museo*, in *Archivi fotografici e arte contemporanea in Italia. Indagare, interpretare, inventare*, proceedings of the conference edited by B. Cinelli, A. Frongia, Scalpendi, Milan 2019, pp. 153–177; *22 marzo 1968 Mario Cresci fotografa "Il Percorso" di Piacentino, Pistoletto, Nespolo, Mondino, Boetti, Merz, Zorio, Anselmo, Paolini allo Studio Arco d'Alibert di Roma*, OkPrint, Rome 2008. Relations with this institution tighten

especially in the Nineties, on the occasion of the anthology of Achille Perilli, and continue with the collaboration of Mara Coccia on the retrospective of *Sonia Delaunay* (2009): See F. Di Castro (ed.), *Achille Perilli. Le carte e i libri 1946–1992*, catalogue of the exhibition (Rome, 18 February – 22 March 1992) (Rome: Carte Segrete, 1992); A. Renzitti (ed.), *Sonia Delaunay Carte dalla collezione della Fondazione Marconi*, exhibition leaflet (Rome, 7 April – 14 June 2009) (Rome: 2009).

6.	See https://www.demarco-archive.ac.uk/ (accessed 30 January 2021). With thanks to Laura Leuzzi for access to the archive material.
7.	Whereas a similar event titled *Milano Punto Uno* takes place at Studio Marconi in Milan from 1 December 1988 to 15 January 1989: See LGN, *Fondi Storici, Mara Coccia*, bundle 24, subfile 1.
8.	LGN, *Fondi Storici, Mara Coccia*, bundle 24.
9.	A. Bain, 'Nuggets of Rome', *The Arts*, February 13, 1989 (LGN, *Fondi Storici, Mara Coccia*, bundle 24, u.a. 2, subfile 1, insert 3).
10.	See C. Henry, *The Arts*, February 24, 1989; E. Gage, 'Miniatures with major ideas!', *The Scotsman*, February 27, 1989; C. Robinson, 'Italian Consul opens exhibit', *The Irish News*, 17 November 1989 (LGN, *Fondi Storici, Mara Coccia*, bundle 24, u.a. 2, subfile 1, insert 3); E. Braun (a cura di), *Italian Art in the 20th Century: painting and sculpture 1900–1988*, catalogue of the exhibition (London, 14 January – 9 April 1989) (London–Munich: Royal Academy of Arts-Prestel, 1989).
11.	See *Roma Punto Uno*, exhibition catalogue, with a text by M. Carboni, Leader Offset, Perugia 1989. The exhibition gathers works by Carla Accardi, Franco Angeli, Gianni Asdrubali, Ubaldo Bartolini, Luigi Boille, Paolo Buggiani, Antonio Capaccio, Tommaso Cascella, Bruno Ceccobelli, Mario Ceroli, Antonio Corpora, Paolo Cotani, Claudio De Paolis, Gianni Dessì, Stefano Di Stasio, Piero Dorazio, Fabbriano Fabbri, Giosetta Fioroni, Andrea Fogli, Mauro Folci, Pietro Fortuna, Enrico Gallian, Paola Gandolfi, Claudio Givani, Valeria Gramiccia, Mimmo Grillo, Piero Guccione, Antonietta Lama, Felice Levini, Giancarlo Limoni, Sergio Lombardo, Carlo Lorenzetti, Enrico Luzzi, Renato Mambor, Graziano Marini, Titina Maselli, Vittorio Messina, Fabio Mauri, Sabina Mirri, Elisa Montessori, Giulia Napoleone, Nunzio, Luigi Ontani, Roberto Pace, Giorgio Pagano, Claudio Palmieri, Achille Perilli, Alfredo Pirri, Vettor Pisani, Piero Pizzi Cannella, Enrico Pulsoni, Remo Remotti, Paolo Ristonchi, Lucia Romualdi, Mariano Rossano, Mimmo Rotella, Francesco Ruggiano, Giuseppe Salvatori, Rocco Salvia, Sergio Sarra, Toti Scialoja, Cesare Tacchi, Nino Scordia, Guido Strazza, Marco Tirelli, Carmine Tornincasa, Giuseppe Uncini, Claudio Verna, Simona Weller, Luisa Zanibelli.
12.	See *Le scuole romane: sviluppi e continuità 1927–1988*, exhibition catalogue (Verona, 9 April–15 June 1988, Milan-Rome, Mondadori-De Luca, 1988); G. Verzotti, *Le scuole romane*, in F.A. Miglietti (ed.), *Arte in Italia 1960–1985* (Milan: Politi, 1988), pp. 41–65.
13.	See LGN, *Fondi Storici, Mara Coccia*, bundle 24, u.a. 2, subfile 1, insert 2, *List of works on show*.
14.	This is the most recurrent solution evidenced by the few photographs in the Mara Coccia Fund at LGN, referable to the Italian venues of the exhibition.
15.	See LGN, *Fondi Storici, Mara Coccia*, bundle 24, u.a. 2, subfile 1, insert 2, *List of works on show*.
16.	See G. Joppolo (ed.), *Forma 1 1947–1987. Accardi Attardi Consagra Dorazio Guerrini Maugeri Perilli Sanfilippo Turcato*, catalogue of the exhibition (Bourg-en-Bresse e Saint-Priest, 13 April – 15 June 1987), (Rome: Christengraf, 1987). The organising committee comprises the directors of the two French museums and Mara Coccia; the scientific committee comprises Joppolo, Gabriella Di Milia and Anne Malochet (authors of the essays in the catalogue); while the coordination of the exhibition and editing of the catalogue are entrusted to Valeria Gramiccia. Among the lenders is also Giorgio de Dominicis, Mara Coccia's partner at the Studio d'Arte Arco d'Alibert, from 1963 to 1970; LGN, *Fondi Storici, Mara Coccia*, bundle 24, u.a. 1.
17.	B. Krimmel (ed.), *Forma 1 1947–1987. Accardi, Attardi, Consagra, Dorazio, Guerrini, Maugeri, Perilli, Sanfilippo, Turcato*, catalogue of the exhibition (Darmstadt, 6 December 1987 – 31 January 1988), (Darmstadt: Mathildenhöhe, 1988). This interest continued later with the collaboration in the project of S. Lux (ed.), *Orientamenti dell'arte italiana. Roma 1947–1989*, catalogue of the exhibition (Moscow, 28 June – 28 July 1989 and Leningrade, 18 August – 17 September 1989) (Rome: Bonanno, 1989).
18.	*Forma 1*, exhibition catalogue (Rome: Arco d'Alibert, 1965). Introductory essay by N. Ponente; report by M. Fagiolo.
19.	See F. Gallo, 'Artisti in video: la serie Nello studio di... dell'Associazione Mara Coccia', *LUK. Quaderni della Fondazione Ragghianti*, 2020, n. 26, pp. 150–160.
20.	In collaboration with the gallery Rive Gauche: a text by Waldemar George appears in Asger Jorn's catalogue; and one by Libero de Libero in Martin Bradley's.
21.	In collaboration with Deutsche Bibliothek Rom: a text by Enrico Crispolti appears in Paul Wunderlich's catalogue.
22.	See LGN, *Fondi Storici, Mara Coccia*, bundle 24, u.a. 2, subfile 2, insert 4. The second edition of *Roma Punto Uno* takes place at Pici Gallery in Seoul, Tokyo Design Center in Gotanda and Kuchu Teien Tenbodai Sky Gallery in Osaka, between September and November 2004: See *Roma Punto Uno*, catalogue of the exhibition with a critical text by M. De Candia (Rome: Gangemi, 2004).

Meikle Seggie:
The Celtic Connection

Adam Lockhart

"What we call the beginning is often the end. And to make and end is to make a beginning.
The end is where we start from."
Little Gidding, T.S. Eliot[1]

Elliot's 1942 poem *Little Gidding* discusses the notions of time, perspective, humanity, and salvation, these concepts have all become important and central to Richard Demarco's beliefs. The poem was written during WWII when Demarco was a boy, a period when a deal of trauma was inflicted upon him both physically and emotionally, it was these days which shaped his future and cemented his life as an artist and explorer.[2]

Origins

The story of Richard Demarco is often blurred between truth and legend, fitting well with his romantic notions of past civilisation and culture. 'To say he would be legendary would be correct' said Scottish artist provocateur, David Mach, 'a rogue … a baroque punk'[3] perhaps emerging from the throes of the Italian Renaissance. A time traveller, taking people from one place to the next with his colourful performative yarns and his epic journeys.

He witnessed the first attack on British soil by the Luftwaffe in WWII in October 1939, when an attempt was made to bomb Rosyth Dockyard and the Forth Rail Bridge. He was playing on Edinburgh's Portobello beach when an RAF Spitfire downed one of the planes.[4] The bullets narrowly missed the young Demarco and his brother, hitting the soft sand around them. But this wasn't the start of this 'friendly fire'. Things took a sinister turn when Benito Mussolini declared war on France and Great Britain in 1940, which resulted in the persecution of Italians throughout the UK. Demarco remembers scenes in Edinburgh where angry mobs attacked Italian businesses across the city with the owners being verbally and physically attacked and having to be escorted to school by the police due to the abuse that he had personally received.[5] The sinking of the Arandora Star ocean liner by a German U-Boat, also had a profound effect on Demarco, it contained 734 Italian civilian men who had been arrested and were being sent to be interred in Canada.[6] Most of these men drowned, including a hundred from Edinburgh. Amongst them were the father and uncle of artist and fellow Italo-Scot, Eduardo Paolozzi.

During his attendances at the Catholic Church during the war, Demarco was struck by the number of new attendees in the congregation. Along with the usual worshippers, he saw the military uniforms of three different countries, British and Polish with Italian prisoners of war. This was a sign of things to come for Demarco who in the future would work extensively to bring the art and culture of these nations together. As a deeply religious person he saw the Catholic Church as his spiritual home, so much so that he almost became a priest.[7] He was equally fascinated by the earlier entity, the Roman Empire, with modern day Poland and Scotland representing its two European extremities in the East and West. These were also the two extremes where Demarco's main sphere of activity and influence were focussed. It was also during this Empire that 'Italian' soldiers were last seen in Scotland. Demarco was fascinated by the fact that these Mediterraneans had come all the way to Scotland, he wondered what they were thinking as they travelled that road.[8] He was also delighted to know that at such a time the Roman empire was, for 2 ½ years, being ruled from the banks of Cramond, now a suburb of Edinburgh, by Emperor Septimius Severus and his son Caracalla who led campaigns to try to subdue the Celts. Roman supply ships would arrive at the mouth of the river Almond at Cramond, where still visible on the beach is the 'Eagle Rock' supposedly carved by the Roman legion based there which Demarco surmises could be the emblem of the 'lost' Legio IX Hispana.[9]

From Cramond and edging further north up to the Grampian mountains, is the place that represents the core of Richard Demarco's existence. It is the frontier where Roman and Celt meet, it is *the Road to Meikle Seggie*. These tensions between Roman (Italian) and Celt persisted for Demarco, even years after the war, both within himself and exter-

nally, making him feel like an outcast for the first 25 years of his life,[10] but despite the legacy of Mussolini and the Axis forces, he was still proud to be an Italo-Scot.[11] He felt that he needed to do something to change the perceptions of Italians in Scotland, he wanted people to know that Italy and Italians were about more than just ice cream parlours and fish and chip shops, but also of the world of the renaissance and Da Vinci. This he endeavoured to do by advancing himself and others through art and education, something he has continued to do throughout his life.[12]

Inspiration

In Demarco's life, there were four defining moments or epiphanies which have carved his career and life. The first of these was the inaugural *Edinburgh International Festival* in 1947. For the 17-year-old Demarco, this was just the tonic he felt Edinburgh needed in post war Scotland. He describes it as 'life changing' as if it 'came down from the sky', almost like divine intervention, 'created by people who loved Europe'.[13] Indeed, this was an ambitious venture only two years after the end of the war. In the words of the then Edinburgh Lord Provost, John Falconer:

> It is an endeavour to find a stimulus to the establishing of a new way of life centred round the arts… and hopes that [the visitors] will find in all the performances a sense of peace and inspiration with which to refresh their souls and re-affirm their belief in things other than material.[14]

These words resonated with Demarco and still do now, even though, in his opinion the festival, has now lost is way through commercialism.

The second epiphany was when he visited Paris for the first time in 1949 and then Rome with his Father in 1950 for the Holy Year, both of which further opened his eyes. He was entranced by the buildings and architecture in Rome, compared with Britain which he thought grubby. His Father said he should be proud to be Roman[15] and through this he recognised that Rome and Italy were still the heart and centre of Europe.[16] On entering St Peter's Basilica in the Vatican, he experienced his first *gesamtkunstwerk* – seeing sculpture, painting, architecture and ritual united on a grand scale. It was seeing the whole experience of these rituals at Christmas and Easter in church in Edinburgh that gave him his abiding interest in theatre and performance.[17] Despite the differences between Italy and Scotland, Demarco discovered and highlighted many comparisons. Edinburgh is often called the 'Athens of the North', Demarco however, '… preferred to think of it as the Northern European equivalent of Rome',[18] both cities being set on seven hills and having similar arterial characteristics – narrow alleyways, pends and steps.[19] He also compares the Italian Renaissance with the Scottish Enlightenment, which is perhaps to do with both countries boasting some of the oldest Universities in the world. Other similarities he noticed were: thinkers Hugh MacDiarmid and Plato, the explorers David Livingston and Marco Polo, innovators Alexander Graham Bell and Guglielmo Marconi, and many others.[20] He saw that these links confirm that the two countries do not have opposing thoughts, but parallels which should be embraced. 'I wanted a mutual dialogue cultivated between Scotland and Italy'.[21]

Again, when Demarco was at Church, they prayed in Latin – which had been the lingua franca of Europe, the language of the Roman Empire.[22] It was fascinating to him that this universal language was still alive, and it made him think about art. 'If people are making art, they are using an international language'.[23] This language of art has come to define his career, something that transcends borders and nationality, an entity that united his beloved Europe.

The third epiphany was when Demarco encountered Joseph Beuys for the first time in Kassel, Germany at *documenta* in 1968, which led to a long-standing relationship and mutual understanding. Beuys' philosophy of every human being an artist, struck a chord with Demarco, this philosophy chimed with his own spiritual beliefs that man is made in the image of God, the great Creator. The former Director of Edinburgh's Fruitmarket Gallery Mark Francis, went as far as to say that Ricky 'saw Beuys as a Christ-like figure'.[24] During the group show *Strategy: Get Arts* at Edinburgh College of Art in 1970, organised by Demarco in collaboration with the Kunsthalle Düsseldorf, Beuys initiated *Celtic Kinloch Rannoch The Scottish Symphony*, a multimedia action comprising of film, audio, performance, and sculpture. This reached the heart of Celtic culture in Scotland and illuminated the origins of the European Celtic people.

Three years before *Strategy: Get Arts* in 1967, an important exhibition was held at the Richard Demarco Gallery – *Contemporary Italian Art*, which also toured within the UK, to the Museum of Modern Art, Oxford and the Ulster Museum, Belfast. This was organised in conjunction with Palma Buccarelli, the Director of the Galleria Nazionale d'arte Moderna in Rome, being the first major contemporary avant-garde art exhibition in Scotland of Italian art, featuring 37 cutting edge artists such as Mimmo Rotella, Piero Manzoni, Jannis Kounellis, Pino Pascali, Alberto Burri and Lucio Fontana. It's hard to believe now but Demarco said of the exhibition that 'no one was interested in the Italian Avant Garde in Scotland'.[25] A report in the *Scotsman* by Sydney Goodsir Smith partially endorsed this, with its relatively offensive title, *Follies in Dotty Show by Italians,* described it as '…exceedingly pretentious tosh…'.[26] However, many letters of complaint in support of the exhibition were received by the *Scotsman* editor and a more favourable review appeared in the *The Herald,*[27] it also received a very healthy 200 visitors per day.[28] Demarco felt that Scotland was many years behind Italy and that he was asking questions that art schools and gallery directors were not asking. The artist and long-time Demarco collaborator, Arthur Watson, said that 'the Scottish art establishment was obsessed with France, [Richard] opened it up'[29] to other ways of thinking. Interestingly an exhibition of Italian Sculpture held at the Scottish National Gallery of Modern Art the year before, again organised with Buccarelli, featuring more established artists, was received more positively. Art historian Laura Leuzzi hypothesises that this may have been due to the presence of a new generation of artists at the 'younger' Demarco Gallery which weren't fully understood or respected at the time.[30] It may also have been due to the imprimatur of a national gallery and more prominent publicity from NGS.

The Richard Demarco Gallery and its predecessor the Traverse Theatre Gallery were based on the principles of the Maison Demarco, the restaurant that Demarco's family ran in Portobello, which was styled as a French salon rather than an Italian cafe. But it still embraced the idea of the Italian 'La Bella Figura', the Demarco Gallery was more like a meeting place or a club embracing Italian coffee culture. Jane MacAllister said that hospitality, public perception and looking after guests was almost as important as the art that was being exhibited.[31] This was a key part of the spirit of Demarco. However, there came a point where the confines of the Gallery were too restrictive for Demarco, it wasn't enough to bring exhibitions to Scotland, he had to be free to travel and make international connections. This could be said to have led to his fourth epiphany, his discovery of *The Road to Meikle Seggie,* which became the defining philosophy in his life and career.

The Journey

Meikle Seggie is an unassuming farm near the town of Kinross, about 20 miles North of Edinburgh. To most people it means very little, but to Demarco it came to be a leitmotif (Figure 1). In the Autumn of 1972, while travelling back to Edinburgh along the road from the farm where he had been drawing, he had an experience which brought together several symbols connected with nature, history, art and the idea of the journey. He described his senses being heightened with a 'fairy tale magic' in the air. The culmination of this was seeing a shape in the clouds over the Forth Road Bridge, 'a golden light… in the shape of an enormous bird – a flying dragon … with two enormous claws stretches (sic) almost as far as its eagle head'.[32] Could this have represented the lost Roman legion, or did it signify St Serf, that Demarco talks about, who slew the Dragon of Dunning?[33] The legend says that St Serf came up from Rome in the 6th c., bringing Mediterranean Christianity to Scotland, and around the same time St Columba brought Celtic Christianity from Ireland, thus bringing another Celtic Roman connection than burns within Demarco's psyche. It was from this that he knew that the doors of the Demarco Gallery were only the beginning of the journey. In real-

Figure 1:
Countess Panza
di Biumo at the
ten-mile marker
on the road to
Meikle Seggie,
Kinross-shire,
Scotland during
Edinburgh Arts
1975.

ity, the *Road to Meikle Seggie* exists on many levels: it is a metaphor for the journey through life, the journey of human existence in conjunction with the natural world. 'Discovering the road was like opening a door beyond which lay the reality of my dreams, of a world beyond the confines of the 20th century … the space in which I would seek freedom from all the restricting linear concepts of time'.[34]

Demarco started organising formalised journeys which he called 'Edinburgh Arts' in 1972 in the spirit of the Bauhaus and Black Mountain College.[35] These incorporated visits to ancient sites, artist studio visits, lectures, workshops and the whole 'Demarco Experience'. They continued each year in Scotland until 1975, when he decided to incorporate mainland Europe into the journey. The financial viability of *Edinburgh Arts* was ensured by the award of college credits from the School of Scottish Studies at Edinburgh University, to the American students who formed the majority of those participating. It was this, along with Demarco's growing international profile

that ensured the success of *Edinburgh Arts*.[36]

In 1320, the *Declaration of Arbroath* was written in Latin by Scottish nobleman and addressed to Pope John XXII. This is well known as an appeal to the Pope asking for recognition of the sovereignty of Scotland as an independent state. However, less known is that it contains a short history of the origins of the Scots, or more accurately the Celts. It describes the journey they took from the Tyrrhenian Sea through Europe and eventually to Scotland. The Celts took this road before the Romans and, confirmed through archaeological evidence, the Neolithic people before them. This same road was travelled by medieval scholars and then as the 'Grand Tour' by people such as Lord Byron and other well-off individuals starting in the 17th century, to seek out European culture and in particular that of the Italian Renaissance. It was this road that formed the basis of Demarco's *Edinburgh Arts* Journeys from 1975–1979. Interestingly, the guides on the Grand Tours were known as 'cicerones' which is derived from Cicero, the Roman

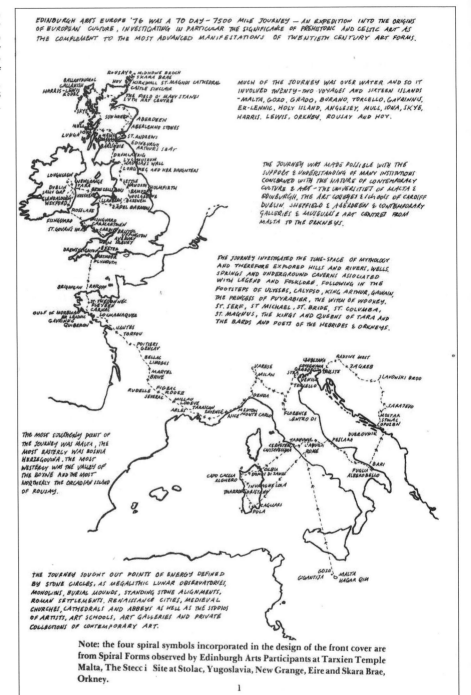

EDINBURGH ARTS EUROPE '76 WAS A 70 DAY - 7500 MILE JOURNEY — AN EXPEDITION INTO THE ORIGINS OF EUROPEAN CULTURE, INVESTIGATING IN PARTICULAR THE SIGNIFICANCE OF PREHISTORIC AND CELTIC ART AS THE COMPLEMENT TO THE MOST ADVANCED MANIFESTATIONS OF TWENTIETH CENTURY ART FORMS.

MUCH OF THE JOURNEY WAS OVER WATER AND SO IT INVOLVED TWENTY-TWO VOYAGES AND SIXTEEN ISLANDS - MALTA, GOZO, GRADO, BURANO, TORCELLO, GAVRINNIS, ER-LENNIC, HOLY ISLAND, ANGLESEY, MULL, IONA, SKYE, HARRIS, LEWIS, ORKNEY, ROUSAY AND HOY.

THE JOURNEY WAS MADE POSSIBLE WITH THE SUPPORT & UNDERSTANDING OF MANY INSTITUTIONS CONCERNED WITH THE NATURE OF CONTEMPORARY CULTURE & ART - THE UNIVERSITIES OF MALTA & EDINBURGH, THE ART COLLEGES & SCHOOLS OF CARDIFF DUBLIN, SHEFFIELD & ABERDEEN & CONTEMPORARY GALLERIES & MUSEUMS & ART CENTRES FROM MALTA TO THE ORKNEYS.

THE JOURNEY INVESTIGATED THE TIME-SPACE OF MYTHOLOGY AND THEREFORE EXPLORED HILLS AND RIVERS, WELLS, SPRINGS AND UNDERGROUND CAVERNS ASSOCIATED WITH LEGEND AND FOLKLORE. FOLLOWING IN THE FOOTSTEPS OF ULYSSES, CALYPSO, KING ARTHUR, GAWAIN, THE PRINCESS OF PUYRABIER, THE WITCH OF WOOKEY, ST. SERF, ST MICHAEL, ST. BRIDE, ST. COLUMBA, ST. MAGNUS, THE KINGS AND QUEENS OF TARA AND THE BARDS AND POETS OF THE HEBRIDES & ORKNEYS.

THE MOST SOUTHERLY POINT OF THE JOURNEY WAS MALTA, THE MOST EASTERLY WAS BOSNIA HERZEGOVINA. THE MOST WESTERLY WAS THE VALLEY OF THE BOYNE AND THE MOST NORTHERLY THE ORCADIAN ISLAND OF ROUSAY.

THE JOURNEY SOUGHT OUT POINTS OF ENERGY DEFINED BY STONE CIRCLES, AS MEGALITHIC LUNAR OBSERVATORIES, MONOLITHS, BURIAL MOUNDS, STANDING STONE ALIGNMENTS, ROMAN SETTLEMENTS, RENAISSANCE CITIES, MEDIEVAL CHURCHES, CATHEDRALS AND ABBEYS AS WELL AS THE STUDIOS OF ARTISTS, ART SCHOOLS, ART GALLERIES AND PRIVATE COLLECTIONS OF CONTEMPORARY ART.

Note: the four spiral symbols incorporated in the design of the front cover are from Spiral Forms observed by Edinburgh Arts Participants at Tarxien Temple Malta, The Stecci Site at Stolac, Yugoslavia, New Grange, Eire and Skara Brae, Orkney.

1

statesman and poet who became an important figure in the 18th century enlightenment, of which Demarco speaks fondly, especially due to Cicero's birthplace of Arpino and his villa in Formia both being located reasonably near to his ancestral town of Picinisco.[37] Demarco, the guide on these trips, would probably enjoy being seen as a modern-day Cicero. Guardian writer, Michael Billington, affectionately calls him 'a supreme cultural bandit'.[38] One can imagine him like Dick Turpin marauding up and down the highways of Europe, but instead of carrying a pistol, he carries a camera, shooting everything and everyone. Terry Ann Newman, Demarco's deputy director, says that his camera helps people to 'up their game and perform',[39] to fully embrace the experience. These photographs have also become important records in themselves, capturing significant moments in cultural history as well as the minutiae of everyday life.

The first of these European expeditions was called *To Callanish from Hagar Qim*, the second *A Journey from Hagar Qim to the Ring of Brodgar*. Callanish being on the Isle of Lewis (Figure 2), the Ring of Brodgar in Orkney (both in the north of Scotland) and Hagar Qim on the island of Malta, which were all sites of significant Neolithic structures. Demarco considered Malta to be part of the extended group of islands that make up Italy.[40] The trips generally took a similar route, mainly taking in Malta, Sardinia, mainland Italy, Yugoslavia, France, the British Isles and always Scotland. The last European trip in 1979 included Greece. True to the Beuys philosophy, the participants in these journeys came from all sorts of backgrounds and nationalities, from artists to farmers, architects, poets, bus drivers, ministers of religion, Canadians, Americans, Italians and Australians, present for all or parts of the trips. The purpose of these trips was to re-connect contemporary art and culture with that of pre-history, showing that art did not begin at the Renaissance, particularly reconnecting Italy with its pre-Roman Celtic, Nuragic and Etruscan past. Demarco highlighted the connections between ancient Mediterranean Europe with Britain and especially Scotland. For example, bringing attention to

links with the Pennines and Cumbria in North England with the Apennines and Umbria in Italy. French art historian Deborah Laks recognises this as '… Demarco's way of shining a light on a pre-European coherence and, in doing so, resituating Scotland at the heart of contemporary, political and artistic Europe'.[41]

For the Demarco the key to unlocking these ancient sites were the Greco-Roman gods Psyche and Techne, representing art and science/engineering. For the ancients these concepts were intertwined, rather than separate as they have generally become today. He related the Celtic Earth Spirit goddess to Psyche, and her consort Lugh as the equivalent of the Roman god Mercury, characterising communication.[42] This 'communication' was evident in the locations of standing stones that were visited, where the ancients built megalithic solar and lunar observatories, perhaps in an attempt to communicate to the spirit world.

On Malta, visits to Hagar Qim, the megalithic temple complex, were imperative along with other similar sites, such as Mnajdra and the Hypogeum of Hal Saflieni. Demarco recognised the significance of these places: 'Hagar Qim, a place to find engineering, sculpture, spirituality and sanctum sanctorum … a place to consider the passing of time'.[43] This passing of time and the cycle of life was linked with the 'spiral', a common reoccurrence throughout these journeys, carved into stone or drawn on walls and found on objects in the various related museums of antiquity that were visited. They also defined the ancients' awareness of the cycle of the sun, moon and stars, electromagnetism, underground springs, solstices, equinoxes, and eclipses,[44] also pre-empting the discovery of galaxies and DNA. He also

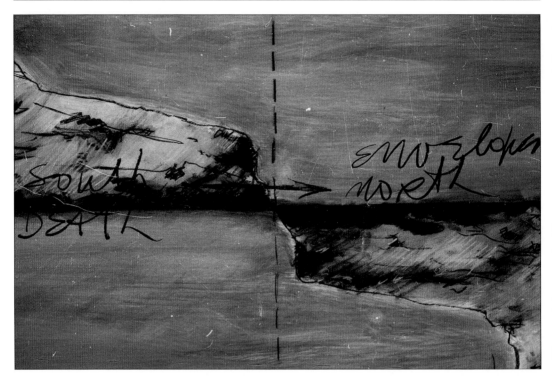

Figure 3: Detail of artwork by Peggy Stuffi and Anselmo Anselmi entitled *Opposites*, at the National Museum of Fine Arts, La Valletta, Malta during Edinburgh Arts 1975.

highlighted the startling similarities of the Hypogeum of Hal Saflieni with Maeshowe Cairn and Midhowe Broch on Orkney, with their alcoves and corridors. His interest in the juxtaposition of art, science and architecture evident in these sites established a long-standing relationship with Maltese architect Richard England, whose signature concrete buildings were influenced by these ancient structures. England would organise the Maltese sections of the tours and

Figure 4: Edinburgh Arts participants at the Bronze Age round tower of Nuraghe Losa, near Abbasanta, Sardinia, 1976.

give lectures on the culture of Malta. During these visits, exhibitions were held at the National Museum of Fine Arts, Valletta, with Italian artists Peggy Stuffi and Anselmo Anselmi collaborating on a piece in 1975, *Opposites* (Figure 3), a diagrammatic series of drawings making comparisons of 'opposites' on the journey, and Anglo-Maltese artist John Borg Manduca who was working with Scottish artist, Ian Hamilton Finlay, exhibited there in 1976. Other actions and performances were held outside, creating a dialogue with the land, such as a video piece by Italian artist Paolo Patelli in 1975. Demarco's influences in Malta extended beyond the journeys, Maltese artist Norbert Francis Attard, stated that his practice was influenced by Scottish artist Dawson Murray who were introduced to each other through Demarco.[45] Such was his impact, that in 1999, on the invitation of the aptly named, Maltese President Guido de Marco, Demarco was invited to be an advisor to help develop the country's cultural strategy. 'Your dreams have reality behind them, more than dreams, ideas, the common heritage of mankind'[46] proclaimed President de Marco.

Sardinia is home to thousands of megalithic sites comprising of standing stones and Nuraghe, the stone towers built by the Nuragic people, reminiscent of Scottish Brochs. Although there is no consensus on the purpose of these buildings, they are thought to be watchtowers or even solar observatories.[47] The Edinburgh Arts groups visited many of these sites at places such as Barumini, Silanus and Sant'Andrea Priu in Bonorva, and again (Figure 4), as they were in Malta, interacting with the environment they found themselves in. On the Italian mainland another Pre-Roman civilisation was investigated, the land of the Etruscans, the southern neighbours of the Celts. The groups were taken to places such as Etruscan tumulus tombs at Cerveteri and to see the Etruscan archaeological artifacts in Tarquinia at the 15th century Palazzo Vitelleschi.

The Italian artist Mario Merz, was one of the main proponents of the Arte Povera movement. As a person who connected to these ancient sites, Merz was an important person to Demarco. In 1976 those on the journey visited the Galleria Mario Pieroni in Pescara, where a Merz

Figure 5: Edinburgh Arts participants with Mario Merz installation based on the Fibonacci sequence at Galleria Mario Pieroni, Pescara, Italy, 1976.

artwork was installed based on the pre- viously mentioned spiral (Figure 5) or more precisely the Fibonacci or Golden Spiral often found in the natural world, named after the 13th c. Italian mathema- tician. This spiral and its manifestation in nature was further investigated by the Scottish mathematician D'Arcy Thompson, forming the basis of his 1917 publication *On Growth and Form*. This work by Merz took the form of a table spiralling through the gallery constructed from steel, stone and glass, with stand- ing stones and leafless twig like branches placed at irregular intervals. On the tabletop, glowing neon tubes dis- played the numbers in the Fibonacci se- quence, creating further electromagnetic

spirals.[48] This work linked directly with nature, science, the ancients and the modern world. Years later in 1988, De- marco brought Merz to the Demarco Gal- lery on Blackfriars Street in Edinburgh enabled by funding from the Scottish Sculpture Trust. Here, he exhibited a similar piece entitled *Tavola,* a more mini- mal work again featuring a curved glass table embedded with slate circles which Merz describes in the exhibition cata- logue as '… like a jewel has its organic point curved, with no geometrical shape. This means that if you continue its lines … it would become a spiral organically, just as leaves and flowers often show the beginnings of thousands of spirals in the universe'.[49] Demarco also led Merz to Achnabreck in the Kilmartin valley, Argyll, Scotland to view the ancient rock carv- ings of cup and ring marks.[50] On this trip a discussion took place with Demarco and Merz for the Murray Grigor directed television programme, *The Demarco Di- mension: Art in a Cold Climate* where Merz explained that these marks were not abstract as Demarco had suggested, but he surmised that they depicted con- centric circles from water droplets into pools. Merz based many of his works on the Fibonacci sequence, but another common element was the dome or igloo, which can be related to the tumuli or earth mounds, which are found all over Europe, which are normally burial cham- bers, therefore signifying the cycle of life and death. His work also references Scottish Neolithic 'Platonic solids', geo- metric stone spheres found in graves carved 1000 years before the time of Plato.[51] In 1978 Edinburgh Arts visited one of his dome artworks at the Venice Biennale. Another example was at the collection of the important art collector Count Panza di Biumo in Varese, an es- sential stopping point on all these jour- neys around Italy.

Figure 6: Jane Chisholm in Bruce Nauman's *Green Light Corridor* installation at the collection of Count Panza di Biumo at Villa Menafoglio Panza, Varese, Italy during Edinburgh Arts 1975.

Count Panza's collection, housed in the Villa Menafoglio Litta Panza, is very significant. It consists of a large number of 20th century artworks by many major artists including numerous minimalist works by artists such as Sol Le Witt, Jene Highstein, Robert Irwin, Bruce Nauman and Jan Dibbets. Arthur Watson (Figure 6), who visited the collection with Demarco, said that there was a whole floor of Dan Flavin's work which was an amazing feat of installation.[52] During the trips Panza would give personal tours of the collection and provide lectures on the works and his philosophical approach to collecting. The minimalist works on display with their geometric shapes and repeated patterns were installed within the architecture of the buildings, linking back to pre-historic constructions. Demarco formed a close relationship with Count Panza, whom he called a 'patron'. They worked together many times over the years, with Panza visiting Scotland on several occasions and participating in sections of the Edinburgh Arts tours. Jane MacAllister said that Panza loved Scotland and the British way of life.[53]

Another patron of Demarco's and a regular stop off on the tours was to the Villa Foscarini Rossi of Luigino Rossi at Stra in the region of Venice. Rossi was the owner of the 'ultra-modern' designer shoe factory, Rossimodo, also near Venice which was usually visited at the same time. At the villa was Rossi's collection of contemporary art and a large collection of designer shoes, both historical and contemporary. Giuliano Gori, another collector often visited, who was based in Pistoia, Tuscany at the La Fattoria di Celle. However, Gori mainly collected outdoor environmental artworks many of which are influenced by the type of Neolithic works visited on the journeys, such as *La cabane éclatée aux 4 salles* (2005) by Daniel Buren, *Labyrinth* (1983)

by Robert Morris and *Catharsis* (1985) by Polish artist Magdalena Abakanowicz, another long-time Demarco collaborator. Although all these works were installed after the Edinburgh Arts trips, there is little doubt that the influence of the trips had a bearing on Gori's collection. Through Demarco, Gori purchased an artwork *The Virgilian Wood* (1985) by the reclusive Scottish artist Ian Hamilton Finlay.[54] Finlay, who also called himself a gardener, had constructed, in collaboration with his wife Sue, his own outdoor environmental artwork, originally called *Stonypath* then renamed *Little Sparta*. The Finlays gradually expanded the garden, reclaiming further tracts of moorland and redesignating the outbuildings of the former farm. Individual poetic sculptures made from a variety of materials were sensitively placed in the landscape devised by the Finlays, executed by a range of skilled collaborators. Common themes are cartesian references, standing stones and carved symbols with text, alluding to the ancient culture of the Celts, the Neoliths and other similar groups in Europe. Interestingly there is a section called the 'Roman Garden'. Count Panza visited Little Sparta many times, due to his interest in Finlay's work and gardens in general. The grounds of Panza's villa already had a 19th century English garden with an aviary and tea house when he originally bought it.[55] *Little Sparta* was another place that the Edinburgh Arts tours visited regularly amongst other artists' studios in Scotland.

In Venice, an important stop was the Galleria del Cavallino, which was run by Gabriella and Paolo Cardazzo, who took over from their father Carlo, described by Demarco as a genius,[56] who founded the gallery in 1942. Demarco started a dialogue with the galleria in 1968, where over the years many fruitful and impor-

Figure 7:
Edinburgh Arts
participants on
the walls of the
Iron Age Broch of
Gurness,
Aikerness,
Orkney, 1976.

tant exchanges were made, acting al-most like a sister gallery to the Demarco Gallery. Exhibitions of Demarco related artists were held at Cavallino and asso-ciated venues, with Cavallino artists exhibited in Scotland. Examples are: *7 Galleria del Cavallino Artists* held at the Royal College of Physicians, Edinburgh in 1974 and *Sei artisti scozzesi (Six Scot-tish Artists)* at Cavallino in 1983. On the Edinburgh Arts trips Cavallino would or-ganise exhibitions and events to coin-cide with the journeys, including boat trips to places not normally visited by tourists and meetings with other galler-ists, such as Guido Parocca, Director of the Museum of Contemporary Art in Venice. As well as organising happen-ings at the galleria, Gabriella Cardazzo was also an active participant in parts of the journeys, regularly travelling to the UK.

From Italy, the journeys could take a detour into Yugoslavia, passing through France, England, Wales, Ireland and eventually to Scotland. Here they would assemble an exhibition of work made on or inspired by the journey. This would be shown during the Edinburgh Festival at the Demarco Gallery or another venue promoted by Demarco. They would then travel out of Edinburgh 'on the road to Meikle Seggie' which could lead to the west coast, up to the north coast via the islands and then back to Edinburgh down the east coast. Along the way they would visit artists' studios, including Ain-slie Yule and Will Maclean, attend ceilidhs, go to artist film screenings by, for instance, Margaret Tait and crucially, visit the ancient sites. The Pictish stones at Aberlemno, the stone circle at Callan-ish and Dun Carloway Broch on Lewis, the Brochs of Gurness and Midhowe on Orkney. Therefore, an opportunity to compare these sites with those visited on the earlier legs of the journey. At the culmination of the eponymous journey in 1976 on Orkney, '... the moon rose obe-diently above the Ring of Brodgar, as it had done over the Maltese equivalent [at] Hagar Qim'.[57] This took place in the presence of the Italians Gabriella Car-dazzo, Anselmo Anselmi and Giorgio Teardo (Figure 7).

Demarco points out that for most

people the idea of a journey has become of secondary importance to the point of arrival, which they view as different from point of departure, but not the view taken by the legend of Ulysses, who he relates to – Ulysses chose the hard road.[58] The journeys took people to places that tourists wouldn't normally visit, focussing on unseen and overlooked places deemed insignificant. They would grant you access to people you wouldn't normally meet where you were thrown into the top level immediately, according to Terry Ann Newman.[59] Arthur Watson said that you would meet more interesting people on one of his expeditions than you'd normally meet in ten years.[60] Lucy Lippard remarked that meeting people on these journeys is as important as the journeys themselves, regarding the stops on the journeys as 'energy points', the same way the standing stone circles were regarded by the ancients.[61] The art critic and Demarco collaborator Cordelia Oliver poignantly describes her experience on trips with Demarco:

> It is a long time since I came to the conclusion that Ricky Demarco's most valuable gift is that of being able to enlarge and heighten experiences, just by being present. To go on a journey in his company is to be forced to sharpen one's sensibilities, to become almost childlike in a way that, unless you fight against it – which is fatal – can be both revealing and rewarding not to say exhilarating.[62]

Interestingly, Jane MacAllister describes the journeys as 'drawing in the landscape', just by being there, moving through the environment and taking in every moment.[63] Jokingly, but also serious, David Mach said that when the Road to Meikle Seggie would travel through a village, there would be a trail of singed earth left behind.[64] Such is the impact of Demarco's relentless enthusiasm and importantly – mark making.

Mark Making

Aside from the journeys, Demarco left his mark in other key Italian exchanges, which link back to his philosophy of the journey. At the Galleria del Cavallino, two exhibitions of Scottish artists took place in collaboration with Demarco. These were the aforementioned *Sei artisti scozzesi (Six Scottish Artists),* presenting Richard Demarco, Will Maclean, Dawson

Figure 8: Iain Patterson with Gabriella Cardazzo and Richard Demarco in Venice during the exhibition *Six Scottish Artists* at the Galleria del Cavallino in 1974. [Courtesy of Iain Patterson.]

Murray, Liz Murray, Jacki Parry and John Taylor in 1983, and *John Knox, Iain Patterson, Ainslie Yule* in 1974. These exhibitions were preceded by *4 Venetian Artists* in 1973 at the Demarco Gallery featuring Anselmo Anselmi, Franco Costalonga, Paolo Patelli and Romano Perusini. Such was the impact of this, the BBC Radio 4, 12 Noon programme described it as a "valuable exercise in foreign exchange… we do not often see contemporary Italian art, so we must thank both galleries concerned for whetting our appetites for more".[65] For Iain Patterson, a participant in the 1974 exhibition, it provided several connections and opportunities for him. Luigino Rossi ended up buying his main painting from the exhibition (Figure 8) and he later purchased two more paintings directly from Patterson to add to his growing collection. Rossi even gave Patterson's wife a pair of designer shoes from the factory. It also started friendships for Iain with Anselmo Anselmi, who he gifted a painting to[66] and Paolo Patelli, visiting each other in the years following in Italy and Scotland.[67] Rossi also bought a work from Will Maclean, one of the artists in the 1983 show.[68] Maclean along with Dawson Murray, had already made their own Italian connections. Dawson Murray had spent two years in the 1960s in Italy where he studied under the painter Giuseppe Santomaso in Venice and travelled throughout the country. Maclean had been at the British School in Rome in 1966 and interestingly was more drawn to the historians and architects rather than the other artists who were there, with whom he visited places like the Etruscan graves and catacombs.

In 1981, Demarco organised a delegation from the UK to meet Count Panza and to view his collection in Varese. As part of the trip, they also visited Baron von Thyssen's more 'traditional' collection in Lugano, Switzerland, near the Italian border. This was a pre-curser to the conference that would follow in Edinburgh, *Towards the Housing of Art in the 21st Century* and its associated exhibition *The Varese Engagement with Modern Art* in 1983. Art critic, Clare Henry who was on the excursion wrote:

> Only Demarco, Scotland's own Pied Piper, could persuade an Italian Count (Panza di Biumo) and a German Baron (von Thyssen) to specially open their doors to the director and the chairman of the Institute of Contemporary Art, the director of BBC's Omnibus, the curator of the Tate Gallery, a film maker, a publisher, four Scottish sculptors, several painters, a Laura Ashley designer, the critics of a number of eminent newspapers and all.[69]

They were also joined in Italy by several international delegates from around the world. Here, Panza explained the philosophy behind his collection 'My collection is a continuation of my mind, the realisation of my conception of life. Art is the communication of an intuition and owning a work of art is a way of having a part in that intuition'.[70]

Two years later the conference was held during the Edinburgh festival over three days, organised by the Demarco Gallery and sponsored by the Azienda di

Figure 9: L-R, Count Panza di Biumo, Arthur Sackler and Richard Demarco at Donaldson's Hospital Building, Edinburgh during *Housing Art in the 21st Century* Conference, 1983. [Courtesy of Clare Henry.]

Soggiorno Varese (via Panza), the then new Channel 4 Television and the Scottish Arts Council. The purpose of the conference was to attempt dialogue between gallerists and architects on the future of exhibiting contemporary art. The conference speakers were of a very high calibre, Arthur Watson who was one of the delegates, describes it as 'frightening' the people that they managed to get.[71] There were directors and representatives (Figure 9) from major international galleries from the UK, US, Germany, Japan, Australia, France and of course Italy. The accompanying exhibition at the Demarco Gallery, which subsequently toured to the ICA in London, showcased several works from Panza's collection including Jan Dibbets, Dan Flavin, Bruce Nauman, Richard Serra and Italians Ugo Mulas and Vittorio Tavernari. Around the same time Panza was holding discussions with various places and galleries with the intention of donating parts of his collection to them, which included Scotland. Enthusiasm from the Scottish art community led to an invitation for Panza to tour some venues with Demarco looking for possible locations for this donation to be housed. These were all historic buildings much like his own. Under consideration were Castle Menzies in Perthshire, Taymouth Castle at Loch Tay, a farmhouse and two castles in Ayrshire, and Donaldson's Hospital Building in Edinburgh which Panza thought was the most suitable, but at the time it was still occupied. This tour culminated in a meeting at the Demarco Gallery with Colin Thomson, Director of the National Galleries of Scotland, and Douglas Hall, Keeper of the Scottish National Gallery of Modern Art, but unfortunately, these plans never came to pass.[72] Instead this part of the collection went to the Guggenheim Museum in New York.[73] Panza's collection is now open to the public and is split between eleven venues across Italy, the US and Switzerland.

When Demarco had his first proper meeting with Joseph Beuys in 1970 at his studio in Düsseldorf, he showed him a series of postcards of the Scottish countryside. Beuys responded "I see the land of Macbeth; so when shall we two meet again? In thunder, lightning or rain?"[74] They did indeed meet again, not long after when Demarco brought Beuys to Rannoch Moor, where later the performance was filmed that became an integral part of his action: *Celtic Kinloch Rannoch The Scottish Symphony*. Rannoch Moor was a perfect counterpoint to the 'blasted heath' where Macbeth met the three witches. A few years later in 1988, this Macbeth connection continued when Demarco, for the Edinburgh Festival, commissioned the Italian theatre company La Zattera di Babele to perform *Towards Macbeth – A Prologue* on Inchcolm Island in the Forth estuary. This was produced in conjunction with Scotland's National Historic Monuments. "I love impossibilities, I love extremes, I love the impossibility of the production of Macbeth in Italian, involving Scottish actors, on the island where Macbeth the play begins".[75] This multi-site performance was an extract of Macbeth, which started at the Demarco Gallery and then continued by bus and sea to the finale on the island itself. It was directed by Carlo Quartucci and Carla Tatò from the theatre company, in conjunction with Scottish actors John Bett and Juliet Cadzow. Performed in both Italian and English it brought together contemporary dance, music, drama and performance art. Sculptures from Italian artists Jannis Kounellis and Giulio Paolini, were also included making it into a *Gesamtkunstwerk*. It was then re-performed at a later date on the mountaintop historic town of Erice in Sicily. The next year a full production of the whole play was planned, however it was pulled at the last minute either due a to lack of funding or illness and replaced by a production put together and directed by John Bett in, remarkably, only 12 days.

The Venice Biennale is of course one of the most important art festivals in world. Demarco has been to them all since 1968, he has also been to every documenta since 1968 and to complete the 'holy trinity', every Edinburgh Festival since the first in 1947 .[76] Great Britain is represented at the Biennale by its pavilion in the Giardini, but since its incarnation it has rarely featured Scottish Artists. In the early days the Scottish Colourists

Figure 10: Installation of David Mach's *Softening the Hardened Hearts of Men*, a series of five elements using photographs of Bonsai trees enlarged to the size of normal trees and bonded to laser-cut steel structures at the Giardini at the 44th Venice Biennale, 1990.

and Charles Rennie Mackintosh were exhibited within larger groupings of British artists. Then in the 1950s Eduardo Paolozzi appeared in a group show. It was due to this disparity that Demarco wanted to make amends.

> The Italian in me has got to get Scotland into the Venice Biennale, my dream is to have a Scottish pavilion... I believe that the most important dialogue imaginable in Europe is that impossible one between north and south, between the Mediterranean and Atlantic between Celt and the Roman.[77]

Through his perseverance and at his instigation, this came to fruition in 1990. It was mainly funded by the Henry Moore Foundation and The British Council, but organised by the Scottish Sculpture Trust (SST) under the umbrella of the Glasgow European City of Culture. The team from SST was led by Barbara Grigor, the trusts chair, and Clare Henry, who sought out suitable venues. Eventually, at the invitation of the Biennale director Giovanni Carandente who was introduced to Demarco via Gabriella Cardazzo, they were given an outdoor area central within the Giardini, adjacent to the American and Italian Pavilions. The artists selected were David Mach, Arthur Watson, and Kate Whiteford for the titular *Tre scultori scozzesi* (Three Scottish Sculptors). Whiteford's *Sitelines* was a large land drawing cast on-site in dark concrete with light gravel. However, only Kate Whiteford's work had Celtic overtones in line with her previous work on Calton Hill, illustrated in the preliminary biennale catalogue. Mach's work, which he described as 'anti-nationalist' *Softening the Hardened Hearts of Men*, featured laser cut steel structures (Figure 10) with images of bonsai trees enlarged to the scale of normal trees. This highlighted opposites, Bonsai trees being small, delicate and Japanese, but here they were large, solid and Scottish. Hence, linking to the opposites of Italy and Scotland. *Across the Sea* by Watson was inspired by the similarities of Venice and Aberdeen, both working ports in the north east of the respective countries and far from their capital cities.[78] The piece consisted of a number of brightly coloured screen-printed fisherman's smocks displayed on a pyramidal structure, almost like ship's sails, responding to Turner's watercolour of *Sunset on the Grand Canal*. Due to problems with customs, Watson's work arrived late, so it was installed during the press opening of the Biennale,[79] so in true Demarco style, the installation became a piece of performance art. The impact of the Scottish exhibition led to Giovanni Carandente writing that he "considered this exhibition among the most important events of the 44th International event".[80] To this day it is the only time Scotland has been represented independently in the Biennale Giardini, taking another 13 years before the next official Scottish exhibition occurred in 2003. This presence has continued ever since but always out with the main site of the Biennale.

The End?

The location of many iterations of the Demarco gallery were near the Worlds End Close off the Royal Mile in Edinburgh. It was called such, due to it being the place where the old city gates stood therefore marking the end of the city. This was often the starting point for *Edinburgh Arts* journeys and the start of *the Road to Meikle Seggie*. As it is the end, it also means the beginning for Demarco – the spiral, the journey, the past and the future. Jane MacAllister noted that he was always ahead of the curve, which can be a lonely place, with the importance of his endeavours not being recognised until years after the event.[81] His mission to re-connect Scotland with Italy and more importantly with Europe, the ancient place of the Neoliths, Celts, Nuraghe, Etruscans and Romans has been fruitful, but there is still a way to go for this to become embedded in the public psyche. The artist Jimmy Boyle described him as "an unrecognised prophet in his own land… unfortunately when he dies it will be then he is recognised".[82]

Demarco's extensive archive will move to Granton under the care of the Scottish National Galleries, to a location very near to Cramond, the place where the Roman Empire was ruled from for those years under Septimius Severus. Thus, the legacy of Demarco lives on at that border of the Celt and the Roman.

"I am only making one exhibition. It continues through time. My artwork is the act of being alive."[83]

Demarco.
The Marker.
Il Marchio.

Endnotes

1. T. S. Eliot, *T. S. Eliot's "Little Gidding"*, 1942 [online]. Columbia.edu. Available at: http://www.columbia.edu/itc/history/winter/w3206/edit/tseliotlittlegidding.html [accessed 21 April 2021].
2. Demarco paraphrases this quote from T.S. Eliot in *Artery: Richard Demarco The Road to Meikle Seggie*, 1999, television Broadcast, Scottish Television.
3. 'Interview of David Mach for Richard Demarco: The Italian Connection', 2019 [online]. Available at: https://vimeo.com/408804291 [accessed 21 April 2021].

4. Sandra Dick, 'How Richard Demarco was almost shot in Nazi raid', *Edinburgh News*, 30 January 2015 [online]. Available at: https://www.edinburghnews.scotsman.com/news/how-richard-demarco-was-almost-shot-nazi-raid-1513999 [accessed 21 April 2021].
5. David McLean, 'Violent anti-Italian riots in Edinburgh recalled 80 years on', *Edinburgh News*, 10 June 2020 [online]. Available at: https://www.edinburghnews.scotsman.com/heritage-and-retro/retro/violent-anti-italian-riots-edinburgh-recalled-80-years-2879748 (accessed 21 April 2021).
6. David McLean, 'Richard Demarco calls for Edinburgh memorial to Arandora Star victims', *Edinburgh News*, 2 July 2020 [online]. Available at: https://www.edinburghnews.scotsman.com/heritage-and-retro/retro/richard-demarco-calls-edinburgh-memorial-arandora-star-victims-290 2230 [accessed 21 April 2021].
7. 'Interview of Jane MacAllister for Richard Demarco: The Italian Connection', 2020 [online]. Available at: https://vimeo.com/671088153 [accessed 28 January 2022].
8. 'Richard Demarco: Italy, Scotland, Europe', University of Edinburgh, 2018 [Audio Recording]. Available at: https://vimeo.com/313206696 [accessed 21 April 2021].
9. Richard Demarco, *Richard Demarco: A Life in Pictures* (Ellon: Northern Books, 1995), p. 28.
10. 'Interview with Richard Demarco, January 2017, Part 1 [online]. Available at: https://vimeo.com/280736033 [accessed 22 April 2021].
11. Demarco, *Richard Demarco: A Life in Pictures*, p. 44.
12. 'Interview with Richard Demarco', part 1.
13. *Ibidem*.
14. John Falconer, *Edinburgh Festival catalogue* (Edinburgh: Edinburgh Corporation, 1947), p. 7.
15. 'Richard Demarco: Italy, Scotland, Europe'.
16. *The Demarco Dimension: Art in a Cold Climate*, 1988 [Television Broadcast]. VIZ for Channel 4 Television.
17. Richard Demarco, *A unique partnership Richard Demarco, Joseph Beuys* (Edinburgh: Luath Press, 2016), pp. 63–65.
18. *Ibidem*.
19. 'Richard Demarco: Italy, Scotland, Europe'.
20. Demarco, *Richard Demarco: A Life in Pictures*, p. 46.
21. *Ibid.*, p. 28.
22. 'Interview with Richard Demarco', part 1.
23. Interview with the Author and Richard Demarco, 2020 [offline audio recording].
24. *The Demarco Dimension: Art in a Cold Climate*, (1988) [Television Broadcast]. VIZ for Channel 4 Television
25. Interview with Richard Demarco', part 1, 2020.
26. Goodsir Smith, 'Follies in Dotty Show by Italians', *The Scotsman*, 20 March 1967.
27. 'Contemporary Italian work on Show in Edinburgh', *The Herald*. 23 March 1967.
28. Report n. 443/815 dated 30/03/1967, signed by Alfredo Trinchieri, Italian Consul General, to the Director General of Culture. National Gallery of Modern Art, Archivio Storico, POS. 9B Mostre fuori galleria 1965–1967, Busta 13, Fascicolo 4.
29. Interview of Arthur Watson and Will Maclean for Richard Demarco: The Italian Connection, 1 August 2019 [online]. Available at: https://vimeo.com/285256135 [accessed 23 April 2021].
30. Laura Leuzzi, 'Edimburgo-Roma 1967, connessioni italo-scozzesi sulle tracce della mostra *Contemporary Italian Art* alla Richard Demarco Gallery', *Storia dell'arte*, 2019, n. 1–2, pp. 205–215. Leuzzi provides an in-depth report on this exhibition.
31. 'Interview of Jane MacAllister'.
32. Richard Demarco, *The Road to Meikle Seggie* (Edinburgh: Luath Press, 2015, 2nd edition), p. 72.
33. Dunning is a small village in Perthshire 10 miles over the hills from Meikle Seggie.
34. Demarco, *The Road to Meikle Seggie*, p. 29.
35. Interview with the Author and Richard Demarco, 2020.
36. Interview of Arthur Watson and Will Maclean.
37. Interview with the Author and Richard Demarco, 2020.
38. *The Demarco Dimension: Art in a Cold Climate*.
39. 'Interview of Terry Ann Newman for Richard Demarco: The Italian Connection', 2020 [online]. Available at: https://vimeo.com/671104612 [accessed 28 January 2022].
40. 'Interview with Richard Demarco', March 2017 [online]. Available at: https://vimeo.com/285256135 [accessed 23 April 2021].
41. Déborah Laks, 'Edinburgh Arts Walking on the Celtic Trail', *Switch on Paper* (Nice: Art et sociétés, 2018) [online]. Available at: https://www.switchonpaper.com/en/geopolitics/belief/edinburgh-artswalking-on-the-celtic-trail [accessed 16 August 2021].
42. Demarco, *The Road to Meikle Seggie*. pp. 31, 37.
43. *Artery: Richard Demarco The Road to Meikle Seggie*, 1999 [Television Broadcast]. Scottish Television.
44. Gaston Bachelard, 'Notes on a Descriptive Phenomenology' in D. Bellman (ed.), *A Journey from*

Hagar Qim to the Ring of Brodgar (Edinburgh: Richard Demarco Gallery 1976), p. 9.

45. *Artery: Richard Demarco The Road to Meikle Seggie* (1999) [Television Broadcast]. Scottish Television.
46. *Ibidem*.
47. Lucy R. Lippard, *Overlay Contemporary Art and the Art of Prehistory* (New York: The New Press 1983), p.115.
48. Richard Demarco,. 21–28 June 5th Section of the Journey, in Bellman, *A Journey from Hagar Qim to the Ring of Brodgar,* pp. 9–10.
49. Mario Merz, 'Tavola', Demarco, *Tavola*, p. 25.
50. *The Demarco Dimension: Art in a Cold Climate*, 1988 [Television Broadcast]. VIZ for Channel 4 Television.
51. Lippard, *Overlay Contemporary Art and the Art of Prehistory*, p. 82.
52. 'Interview of Arthur Watson and Will Maclean'.
53. 'Interview of Jane MacAllister'.
54. 'Interview with Richard Demarco', January 2017 Part 2 [online]. Available at: https://vimeo.com/280736033 [accessed 22 April 2021].
55. 'Interview with Richard Demarco'.
56. *Ibidem*.
57. Richard Demarco, '31 July – 5 August 12th Section of the Journey Inverness the Orkney Isles Caithness', in: Bellman, *A Journey from Hagar Qim to the Ring of Brodgar*, p. 153.
58. Demarco, *The Road to Meikle Seggie*, p. 5.
59. 'Interview of Terry Ann Newman'.
60. 'Interview of Arthur Watson and Will Maclean'.
61. Lippard, *Overlay Contemporary Art and the Art of Prehistory*, p. 132.
62. Oliver, C. *The Road to Meikle Seggie Drawings by Richard Demarco* [Exhibition review], unknown publication p. 4.
63. 'Interview of Jane MacAllister'.
64. 'Interview of David Mach for Richard Demarco: The Italian Connection', August 2019 [online]. Available at: https://vimeo.com/408804291 [accessed 21 April 2021].
65. *Twelve Noon 4 Dec 1973*, 1973, BBC Radio 4 Scotland. Transcript available in Scottish National Gallery of Modern Art archive GMA/A37/1/1/659.
66. Gabriella Cardazzo, Letter to Anne Goring, 6 October 1975. Held in Scottish National Gallery of Modern Art Archive GMA/A37/2/104/6.
67. 'Interview of Iain Patterson for Richard Demarco: The Italian Connection', 2019 [online] August. Available at: https://vimeo.com/425874053 (accessed 23 April 2021).
68. 'Interview of Arthur Watson and Will Maclean'.
69. Clare Henry, 'Private re-collections', *The Herald*, 20 October 1981.
70. *Ibidem*.
71. 'Interview of Arthur Watson and Will Maclean'.
72. Richard Demarco, Email to the Author, 16 April 2021, unpublished.
73. 'Interview of Clare Henry for Richard Demarco: The Italian Connection', 2020 [online]. Available at: https://vimeo.com/671097684 [accessed 238 January 2022].
74. Demarco, *A unique partnership Richard Demarco, Joseph Beuys*, p. 38.
75. *The Demarco Dimension: Art in a Cold Climate*, 1988 [Television Broadcast]. VIZ for Channel 4 Television.
76. Demarco, R. (2020). *Interview with the Author and Richard Demarco* [offline audio recording]; and Demarco, R. (2017). *Interview with Richard Demarco March 2017* [online]. March. Available at: https://vimeo.com/285256135 [accessed 23 April 2021].
77. *The Demarco Dimension: Art in a Cold Climate*.
78. *Saturday Night Clyde*, 1990 [Television Broadcast]. BBC Scotland.
79. *Ibidem*.
80. Barfoot, Whiteford, Mach and Watson in Clare Henry (ed.), *Scotland at the Venice Biennale 1990 A Visual Anthology Documenting a Historic Event in Scotland's History* (Glasgow: Clare Henry, n.d.), p. 3. Available at https://pixelbeans74679275.files.wordpress.com/2021/05/venice1990 guideofficial.pdf [accessed 14 July 2022].
81. Interview of Jane MacAllister.
82. *The Demarco Dimension: Art in a Cold Climate*.
83. 'Interview with the Author and Richard Demarco'.

6

The audiovisual and dramaturgical landscape of Carlo Quartucci and Carla Tatò. The experience of La Zattera di Babele

Marco Maria Gazzano

In much of the world today, artistic and critical-theoretical research relating to cinema and audiovisuals move in the direction of interplay and intermediality rather than simple replacement of one technology ('cinema': chemical/optical/mechanical) with another ('cinema': analogue electronic or digital). This is one way among others to enhance rather than remove the technical-aesthetic experiences already acquired historically.

We are moving towards a 'strong' – that is, conscious – integration of technologies and languages. We are heading towards an interaction in dynamic equilibrium between the enhancement of specific audiovisual and of their stories and expressive possibilities. With the inevitable (and productively creative) contemporary trend towards the interplay and mutual extension of technologically determined media and languages (of image and sound), we arrive at new forms of imagination and new "cinematographic" products (artworks?): Scenic, televisual, performative, and more. And

they will no longer be – nor could they be – "spectacles" as we have understood them thus far.

New technologies are needed for *another* "cinema" (and for another "theatre", for another "television", perhaps for another "web") and above all for new and courageous creative imaginations. As well as suitable readiness and sensitivity of creative and productive thought.

Not many artists in the world demonstrate – in their works even more than in their, albeit precise, statements of poetics – an explicit awareness of this trend and its technological, aesthetic, linguistic implications and – why not? – policies. Woody and Steina Vasulka, Katsuhiro Yamaguchi, Nam June Paik, Gianni Toti, Bill Viola, Maria Klonaris e Katerina Thomadaki, Robert Ashley, Zbigniew Rybczyński, Alejandro González Iñárritu, Robert Cahen, Gary Hill, Antoni Muntadas for example, share this line of research with different but equally decisive approaches and outcomes for contemporary culture – and not only for audiovisual culture. Among them, and in this vein, Carlo Quartucci (1938–2019) was one of the first and still is, in his choices, among the most radical: an authentic monument of Italian and European culture still little recognised.

Artist-explorer, like every contemporary 'artist', of media and languages, of aesthetic solutions, of technological 'possibilities', Quartucci offers – with his works, his 'travels', his 'dramaturgical workshops', his 'landscapes' and his poetic declarations – one of the most original (and authentic) possibilities for verifying advanced critical positions. Critical positions that translate into states of theory as well as concreteness in use (or reuse or discovery) of contemporary media, languages of art and communication.

His own concept of 'dramaturgy' is an indication and testimony of this. "Dramaturgy" is understood as *dramaturgy of the arts*, as "the need to write for the stage, creating a state of connivance of arts and artists, intertwining and extending different languages".

This 'state of connivance' between word, music, image, theatre, body, technologies; and artists and arts of all geographical-cultural origins and discipline has its beginnings in the name of Beckett and with the historical avant-gardes (since 1958 and beyond) at the Laboratorio di Camion (1970–1988). It moves from Progetto Genazzano (1980–1985) to documenta 7 in Kassel (1982), from Rome and Paris to Le Giornate delle Arti in Erice in Western Sicily (1989–1992), with an important stop at the Edinburgh International Festival, and with Carla Tatò invited by Richard Demarco (*Towards Macbeth – A Prologue*, August–September 1988) and then Teatr'Arteria again in Rome after 2000. As many paths unravel through the extraordinary 'journeys', some decade long, of Carlo Quartucci around Kleist and Pirandello, Shake-speare and Marlowe, the classical and the modern Myth, the echo of Barbarism, of the Archaic, and the fascination with Contemporaneity. A poetics of places, as well as of figures ('Notes for an imagined artwork between the coasts of Scotland and those of Sicily') has always been (perhaps above all), counterpoint, displacement; 'workshop', and with the energy of decisive reciprocal creative extensions of the tools and languages of art; 'Laboratory' of healthy disorientations, of 'explorations' in fact, towards new points of view. And in sixty years of directing, painters and playwrights, composers and actors, dancers and mimes, photographers and filmmakers have been forced, on entering into a relationship with Carlo Quartucci and Carla Tatò, to face the aporia of their own reassuring professional and disciplinary cages. This also happened – with disruptive effects – to established institutions of today's 'mode of production' of culture: to theatre as well as television, to radio as well as criticism ... And obviously, to Texts, programmatically (and, also, instinctively) removed from consolidated stereotypical interpretations: turned upside down, crossed and "staged" in a set that for Quartucci is also 'image', 'music', 'film', 'video', 'magnetic tape', 'radio', 'TV', 'landscape', 'journey', 'sound', 'actor', 'traveller' ... All done with a precise awareness of how peregrine is every present-day attempt to approach the great Texts/Figures/Myths of theatre and culture that is not interpretative and alienating. This point of view is not only interdisciplinary *ante litteram*, but also a precursor of transculturality and/or *global multimedia films* of the current audiovisual landscape.

Progetto Genazzano, the international meeting of artists in the 1980s, was conceived by Carlo Quartucci and Carla Tatò. It was this and much more: theatre as art and synthesis of the arts – technological and otherwise, made in an extended "set", in different "landscapes" and "airs" – metaphorical and otherwise.

The meeting of artists included painters (Daniel Buren, Giulio Paolini, Per Kirkeby, Jannis Kounellis, Lawrence Weiner, Enzo Cucchi, Jan Dibbets, Luciano Fabro, Markus Lüpertz, Mario Merz, Hermann Nitsch, David Salle), playwrights (Mino Blunda, Roberto Lerici, Aurelio Pes), musicians and video artists (Marina Abramović, Robert Ashley, Henning Christiansen, Massimo Coen, Kit Fitzerald, Joan Jonas, Peter Gordon, Giovanna Marini, Amos Poe, Ulay, Giancarlo Schiaffini, 'Blue' Gene Tyranny, Luigi Cinque, Vittorio Gelmetti), actors and theatre figures (Mimmo Cuticchio e l'Opera dei Pupi, Italian and French circus families, trapeze artists, dancers) critics, organisers and promoters of culture (Guido Aristarco, René Block, Ferruccio Marotti, Marina Bistolfi, Germano Celant, Rudi Fuchs, Marco Maria Gazzano, Carlo Quartucci, Carla Tatò); by means of complex and spectacular high-level projects carried out between Berlin, Rome, Paris, Vienna, Amsterdam, Turin, Chicago, Budapest, Belgrade, Western Sicily, Scotland, New York. Year after year, a theoretical position and a way of being has grown – in theatre and art today, at an international level – peculiar to this group of artists. Virtually two entire generations of the international avant-garde are represented in it: and as stage (or set) the world!

This way of being looks, as Quartucci argues, 'at the interplay of languages for a new dramaturgy of the arts'.

This dramaturgy, while continuing to consider theatre as the privileged centre of attraction for other arts and other languages, knows well how technological innovations, and electronics in particular, are able to enliven, modify the traditional theatrical and artistic environment. A dramaturgy that is convinced of how the rigid division between arts has not reflected, for some time now, the creativity of artists nor the objective reality of their research; and that also knows how much the languages available to artist have multiplied – like the possible 'spaces' of the theatre, on the other hand, from stage to open sea – and how much they can interact and mutually extend – on stage, in video, on magnetic tapes, between media, digitally, in musical composition – their expressive possibilities.

'Theatre as a great regenerating mother of all the arts', writes Carlo Quartucci: evocation/revelation/re-actualization of the Myth, also of that of the Theatre, of the unitary language of art (of the arts), of that *eutopia* of the 'new cities in which artists can live and work' as Rudi Fuchs happily hypothesized in Genazzano in 1983.

This is a theatre of utopian places of 'encounters between artists and arts' (Camion (Truck), La Zattera di Babele, le Giornate delle Arti, the Edinburgh Festival, Cinema, TV, University, Teatr'Arteria …) built on a 'poetic map of the world' evoked by Marcel Broodthaers in 1968 by displacing the usual 'political map of the world'.

This theatre takes place in concrete 'physical' places transfigured and conceptually interpreted into 'mental' places, into 'arias' that produce 'works' – arias also in an operatic sense, the specific cultural 'air' of each landscape – 'Projects', 'workshops': the Truck, Sicily, Genazzano, Scotland, Rome, Berlin, the great contemporary art exhibition, the industrial warehouse, the television studio, the audio recording room, the film set, urban spaces, the fishing port, the Greek temple, the video set, the motorway, the truck bed, the hamlet, the awning, the abandoned farmhouse, the virtual space suggested by the computer, the actual stage.

Places chosen to 'stage' not so much and not just Beckett / Kleist / Pirandello / Melville / Defoe / Omero / Euripide / Marlowe / Shakespeare / Saffo / de Sade / Cervantes / Ibsen / Mozart / Molière but – in this case too – the conceptualisation, for what is possible, of the 'thought' of these authors: the 'beyond oneself' (Marcel Proust 1922) of these Figures, not by chance often presented by the director, on stage and off stage, as real Characters (when not actually intended as real 'traveling companions' of the director and his collaborators). These figures interact, on stage and off stage, with their own texts, with their own characters; and with the poetic choices of the author-director-'orchestrator', who unusually, with his own suggestions, 'puts them on stage'.

This is certainly a non-narrative and non-naturalistic theatre, 'epiphanic' in the sense given to the term by James Joyce in his early writings of 1912 – that is, a theatre capable of making 'visible' what apparently, at first sight, is hidden from the gaze – a theatre aimed at 'staging' (at 'making clear', as far as possible, with art mediums mediated by theatre) that 'beyond' (indicated by Luigi Pirandello in 1915) of the authors themselves and of their subjective perception of reality, lumped in their rockier texts. This theatre is in constant tension towards the 'surreality' (Alberto Savinio, André Breton) of the texts and of those who 'read' them or "listen" to them today in search of the contradictions and vitality of the contemporary. Included in this 'surreality' are the 'public' the 'society of spectators', also considered by Quartucci as a "character" and "actor" no less relevant than those who act on stage. So too, on the other hand, is the 'society of artists'. So too are the languages, ma-chines, technologies, minor roles up to technical-operational and organizational ones – everything that contributes to the unveiling of the 'work' and the realisation of the Project.

This is an *intermedial* 'theatre' by definition, in reciprocal extension and in the evident expressive interaction of the materials and languages assembled. This is an 'open' and perpetually *in fieri* theatre, a 'laboratory' (not simply 'experimental''' theatre) – despite the decisive and solid 'landings' – like the texts of the Authors who are privileged from time to time and in which it is refracted. This theatre is expressed in 'works' (including artworks by design and rigorously, since the 1960s, *site specific*) that are also 'works in progress', 'workshops', 'journeys', 'laboratories', 'factories': always interdisciplinary, often carried out in multi-annual phases, in 'pieces', progressively approaching the text itself, always made in collaboration/ counterpoint/clash/unstable balance with other arts and other artists.

This theatre of progressive sedimentation works in accordance with the main assumption of the international avant-garde (Nouvelle Vague, Informal, Arte Povera, Conceptual, Fluxus, etc.) of which the work of Carlo Quartucci has been a constitutive part since the 1950s: that according to which the 'process of approach' to the 'work' – and the 'works-fragments'/'studies' that derive from it – are (artistically, creatively and as a result) as relevant as the final 'work' itself, if not beyond.

However, in this poetics of 'pieces', of 'steps', of 'fragments' – of 'gleanings' of texts or images, as Agnés Varda would say: of their topical, significant moments, capable of overcoming the present and of helping to define it – which is not exclusive to Quartucci but which finds a particularly rigorous and significant representation in Quartucci's work – there is also another awareness: awareness of language.

An awareness for which (as the psychoanalyst and semiologist Julia Kristeva maintains) the hypnotic rapidity of the image begins to engulf the civilisation of the Word, which the development of technologies causes to sink into thought-calculation; while, on the other hand, hyperconnectivity would feed, on the contrary, on 'elements of language' or 'flashes of inner experience'. Evidence of a humanity to be saved: between the interstices of marketing or the flatness of screens.

And, furthermore, awareness of *catastrophe*: of the sense and perception of the impending catastrophe – accompanying the idea of *progress* – looming in all the poetics of the Western artistic and philosophical avant-garde of the last three centuries. Jannis Kounellis notes in a Round Table of Progetto Genazzano in 1981: "It is probably true – there is a general catastrophe, because it is not explained otherwise how everyone is on La Zattera (Raft). We have a tragedy in mind, and here we want to represent that tragedy of ours and, in fact, we make everyone participate in this, because beyond being our tragedy, it is also a Western tragedy, and therefore it represents itself". On the other hand, Giulio Paolini questions the "politics of appearance" as early as that year, which – thanks to the indiscriminate use of new media, has established itself right up to today and contemporary *social media*: 'If – writes Paolini – "in politics what appears is discourse, but what makes it appear, is the politician as a being", then in art what does not appear is (I did not say that what appears is not)'.

Fragments to face the catastrophe, therefore, and 'explosions' – not only epiphanic and part of 'works in progress'

of contemporary literary ancestry – but also as awareness of "tremendous questions" posed by reality to art and artists today. 'Catastrophe' – at least in the consciousness of Quartucci and his meeting of artists – is not usually understood as an allegory of the 'crisis' and confusion of languages, but more dramatically – in fact – as proven and progressive *powerlessness of art* and the authenticity of self-awareness. *Krisis* which, for the Italian philosopher Massimo Cacciari, since the 80s, is to be understood not as alienation, but as the culmination of a process of knowledge: as a turning point.

These are 'Strong', meaning significant, arguments of that philosophical thought which, starting from the 1970s, in France Jean-François Lyotard called 'postmodern' and in Italy Gianni Vattimo and Mario Perniola indicated as 'weak thought'. A thought that is certainly not 'in crisis' or weak or confused, but more and more conscious – on the wave of the non-ideological reinterpretation of Heidegger and Nietzsche – of the 'forms' necessary for the interpretation of a complex and programmatically evolving contemporaneity, perpetually 'in transition'. It means that no form of thought (and art, or 'form' of the work of art) is able to express an absolute Truth, as metaphysics claimed. It also means that there is no Absolute which, as the Platonic-Aristotelian tradition assumes, can be thought of as the cause of being and as the foundation of morality. This relatively new thought brings with it a relevant consequence: that, if absolute truths are no longer admitted, humanity needs to be rethought beyond human beings as they are today. It is necessary to rethink humanity imagined at the top of the hierarchy of being, to which the dominion of the Earth has been assigned in favour of a human being immersed in the world, in a specific historical epoch, between cultures and traditions that condition them: forced to compare their own vision of the world in a continuous dialogue with the vision of the world of others. And all this with respect for others – whether animate or inanimate – and consequently respect for memory, cultures – even ancestral or minority cultures – diversity, ecology.

This is also the meaning of Carlo Quartucci's 'theatre' since the 1950s: "The idea is to escape a definition of style, the problem of all arts within their historical conventions. Style, its static form, prevents movement; and the great role of the avant-garde consists in moving and fighting the immobile centre of culture", writes Rudi Fuchs for Progetto Genazzano.

Hence, at the beginning of the 1980s, the strong metaphor of a 'Babel' of languages and arts emerges, and in particular that, even more dramatic, of 'La Zattera' (Raft) of artists and of the languages of artists in the storm. This is already an 'answer' in fact that does not hide the drifting of the very foundations of the Modern. A "Project" that is, like the others, "open"; a "response in progress" and at the same time a challenge – of reason, of will, of the "passion of love" – to the world of art and of theatre, to the society of entertainment as well as to that of politics and the media.

The international art critic and *curator* Rudi Fuchs interprets it as a declaration of poetics – in Genazzano in 1981 – very close to the concept of *intermediality* as defined by Dick Higgins in 1966. This theoretical and poetic proposal is shared by Carlo Quartucci and Carla Tatò: "The journey is irregular and uncertain, as in entering Gibraltar, in the chaotic ocean. But each episode leads to the next, bringing with it memories, experiences and suggestions to develop the following one.

The purpose is clear. What happens when a voice enters the image and when the image follows the music and when the music absorbs the image and the actor expresses the poetry in the image?

Poetry gives voice to the image. Music gives melody to poetry. Painting gives an image to music. Dance gives shape to the voice and the voice echoes the image."

Fuchs again writing about "Mutual contemplation" between theatre and other arts, always during Progetto Genazzano, problematizes his own position:

My experiences with La Zattera di Babele convinced me, an idealist, of the immense difficulty of any artistic collaboration. The separation of the arts, born in the nineteenth century but turned into a convention in our century, has become the principle and Leitmotiv of every art. Commingling is possible only under certain, precise conditions of, let's say, equilibrium. The fact that this equilibrium is only ever achievable with great difficulty is demonstrated by almost any attempts of effective collaboration between two or more "autonomous" arts in our century. In most cases, one art becomes a slave to the other art. This becomes more evident where artists collaborate with architects. In spite of this, attempts have always been made.

A similar attempt is also the feat of the La Zattera di Babele. [...] Nothing in art is random, everything is the result of a desire for development and adventure. [...]

Theatre as an alternative to work in the museum and gallery, by which museum rooms are used not only as a neutral place to go through and look at, but as an active scenic place. This means that the museum room is not a static place, but a mobile space that is arranged and articulated around the works of art. [...] The journey in theatre corresponds to a similar mutation of place: perhaps idealized by my own dissatisfaction with the conventional spaces of museums that resemble each other all over the world and everywhere start from the same perceptual formulas.

My hope is a contamination with the theatre, where space immediately passes time and movement and sound can offer new stimuli to the museum. […] in Quartucci's traveling theatre, without a precise space and without a precise image, artists found a workplace full of exciting possibilities: possibilities linked to the word and to music and to movement. In a theatre understood as space and event, the artist's work can become more radical.

Quartucci interpreted all of this as a *dramaturgy of arts*:

There is no need to limit theatrical thinking. Theatre is a magnetic tape, it is a cinematographic projection, it is a musical fact […] There is a written dramaturgy, designed for the stage, there is a musical dramaturgy, there is a visual dramaturgy […] Sometimes I'll use the term *partitura* (score).

'*Partitura*': in Quartucci's language it is both 'music sheet' and 'departure', orchestration of the direction and the beginning of a journey, "script" and *Ouverture*. But it also means "sequence" in the sense of cinema, and – obviously – "montage": juxtaposition/intertwining /creative clash of expressive elements, of specific arts, artists, languages.

A '*partitura*'. Sometimes it is a text, sometimes a 'landscape', sometimes a colour or a sound, sometimes a gesture, sometimes a Figure, sometimes an image. Always an emotion. It is always transformed into a 'scenic body', into a 'dramaturgy'. The collaboration and the dialectic with non-theatrical artists (painters, musicians, dancers, poets, critics, acrobats, filmmakers, performers, etc.) serves precisely this purpose, to extend a concept or an emotion into a 'dramaturgy' with the contribution of the various mediums, of the various experiences, of the various languages, of their reciprocal expressive possibilities.

Quartucci's 'theatre' is, effectively,

even when he does not look directly at cinema, a continuous *framing*: in the Ejzenštejnian sense of 'organization of action and performance within a specific frame […] staging within a frame' (SM Éjzenštejn, *Montaz 1938*).

It is not only 'montage' inside the frame, therefore, as a visual fact, but a real 'staging' of bodies and actors, objects and lights, sounds and gestures, balances and perceptions, of images and other images. For Quartucci, given the profound and complex relationship that in sixty years of directing he established with cinema – and with painting, as evidenced by his use of light, on stage as in video works (you really need to have seen him at work, Carlo, acting *live* between consoles and spotlights and filters, extraordinary performer of light composed *in situ* and live, an authentic painter of light!) – we can talk about a *staging of the image*. We can talk of staging a complex image, which interacts (in a 'montage', in fact) in the large panel of the proscenium-screen (or proscenium-frame?), Summoning a large part of the pictorial, acoustic, gestural, acting, musical most advanced contemporary sensibility. Lesson and result are even more evident in Quartucci's *videos*, since the first *Don Quixote* and *Moby Dick* – revolutionary (and not only for Europe) for the use of colour, *chromakey* and of acting in a non-narrative key.

In fact, video, precisely because of its flexibility, its 'tactility' and the relationships it maintains with painting, brings back – even more than film – Quartucci's framing to its essence of 'image', enhancing it in its many internal 'explosions'.

Video is seen as cinema (scene, theatre, performance…) in the electronic age and 'Figures in an electronic field' his characters, who 'move between parallel screens and monitors in a conceptual montage: but they are still fragments of an artwork. Will they ever, however, be locked into *one* artwork, given the very nature of electronics and the sign of our work?' Quartucci and Tatò ask during Le Giornate delle Arti in Erice in 1986. Not only intersection and extension of languages that are *other*, but also, constitutionally, *vision and audio-vision*.

Carla Tatò, co-creator of La Zattera di Babele – and later Teatr'Arteria – and other Quartucci projects (including educational ones) – already famous for her masterful interpretations of Nora Helmer, Dido, Penthesilea, Medea, Lady Macbeth, energetically puts the emphasis on sound and on the expressive need of vocality:

'The sound-body of the voice, sculpted in the space of the body of the word, by a score of shots sharp, rounded, slipped, pounded by glottis or diaphragm slashes …'. All to be able to convey thoughts themselves with the pleasure of music, beyond words, as Kleist would have wanted.

An idea of a *dramaturgical body* understood as mobile (in motion), plastic and almost as material 'to be sculpted'. Thus, in the expression often used by the Maestro, of the "actor's body", there is certainly the physical presence of the actor on stage in all of its non-removed materiality; but there is also, and overwhelming, the 'physicality' of the word, the voice, the timbres – the modulations of sounds as well as bodies. In this theatre, so bound to the image, the *dramaturgical body of the word* often corresponds to the *dramaturgical body of the scene*. This explains, among other things, the extraordinary radio successes ('acoustic art') of Quartucci, and the great charm of his audiovisual counterpoints.

Achilles, Penthesilea, Nora Helmer, Didone, Lady Macbeth, Tamburlaine, Medea, Cotrone the wizard, Godot, Qui-

xote, the Giants of the Mountain: today, travel companions.

Genazzano, Erice, Scotland, Berlin, the Orient, the Americas, their people: 'they exist firstly as a poetic act, as a conscious and unconscious cultural force that has unleashed the fantastic in us' wrote Carla Tatò in 1988.

The fantastic read as immaterial scene even when it is apparently material. Place of the mind. Imagination 'Such stuff as dreams are made of', as Shakespeare indicated in a very famous verse in *The Tempest* in 1610.

In this irregular and uncertain journey, 'as in entering Gibraltar, in the chaotic ocean', in 1988 the poetic and imaginative project for Edinburgh – entirely dedicated to William Shakespeare – was in many ways decisive. The evocative (interior and beyond) 'landscape' echoes between western Sicily and Scotland, suggested by Richard Demarco as a viaticum to the invitation, also contributed to this.

On this experience, we report an unpublished *a posteriori* testimony by Carla Tatò in dialogue with Marina Bistolfi, the organiser of the international events of La Zattera di Babele.

The protagonist of this conversation is, in addition to the memory of the participants, the Catalogue *Towards Macbeth. A Prologue* curated by the Richard Demarco Gallery in collaboration with La Zattera di Babele for the 1988 Edinburgh International Festival. The catalogue, specifies Carla Tatò, is intended, even before being edited, just as a 'script', which is formed and is being formed little by little: 'for me very important precisely for the approach, for the tale in the images and in the words, for its format, for the writings that have accompanied us and for a dramaturgy that is also directly in the book'.

The conversation between Carla

Tatò and Marina Bistolfi took place in a post-pandemic video web call between May and June 2021.

C. T: We were, at the beginning of 1988, at the Colombaia in Trapani during Le Giornate delle Arti, and a man, (Richard) Demarco, arrived, I don't know from which road, but he arrived at the Colombaia. And this image of the Colombaia immediately put us in a state of frequency, closeness, harmony with him. So, something began that then translated into a journey, a going, a wealth of thoughts, annotations, fragments. About *Macbeth*. About what? Not 'the text', even though we were working on it. We watched all the *Macbeths*, from Orson Welles to Akira Kurosawa (Toshirō Mifune), from Vittorio Gassman to Carmelo Bene: we know them, we studied them we knew them. But what determined the journey was the consonance, and not just the proximity, between that image of the Castle of Sweno and the Colombaia in Trapani. Two precise images, which open the Catalogue *Towards Macbeth. A Prologue*. When we arrived at Sweno Castle, we realized that it really exists.

And the theatrical journey and beyond, around it, we recount it right in the Catalogue: in flashes, in fragments, in splendours. A beautiful journey that I remember making with the extraordinary Richard Demarco in his green Jaguar, in 1988, next to his first wireless phone: huge, large, heavy, black, fascinating suitcase, which looked like a telephone from the Second World War.

Demarco then accompanied us to the famous forest near the Castle, which is the 'witches' forest'. We saw those stone buildings, with a cross at the end

Figures 1a,b:
From the left,
John Bett, Carlo
Quartucci, Juliet
Cadzow and
Carla Tatò,
Inchcolm Island,
1988.

95

Figure 2: Juliet Cadzow and John Bett. Inchcolm Island, 1988.

Figure 3: From left Marina Bistolfi, Carla Tatò and Frank Dunlop, Inchcolm Island, 1988.

fascinated, because the beginning of *Macbeth* with those witches – which translated into Italian was only an attempt at a rhyme – instead it is the Shakespearean *'blank verse'*, so fascinating when listened to in English. So much so that we said to ourselves 'There is a secret in this forest!'. Then we continued to follow our Richard (Demarco) and into every tree, and every square, and every time this little stone pyramid appeared it was a shock to me, because I found there all the studies that we had carried out and about which we no longer needed to think so much, but simply to do. So we began to embark on other trips inside Sweno Castle.

M. B: I found the letters from (Richard) Demarco, from January 1988, who invited you to represent this event, after speaking with the Director of the Italian Cultural Institute in Scotland. And he writes, happy: 'You will be delighted to know the theme of the Festival is *The Kingdom of the two Sicilies*'. The theme of the 1988 Edinburgh Festival was, in fact, the Kingdom of the Two Sicilies. Demarco invited Rudi (Fuchs) and I think the suggestion of the invitation to La Zattera came from these two presentations.

and the name of a woman, almost always Italian. They were images somehow bare, deep, because they let you imagine what had happened before arriving at that small pyramid of stones with a cross and the inscription of the name and the year. I remember that both Carlo (Quartucci) and I were very impressed and

Then there is the copy of a letter of mine that I wrote to him in February, in your name, in which I spoke about what you see in the Catalogue, which is the journey, that is the desire to combine the islands, the islands of Sicily and the islands of Scotland, the Festival dedicated to the two Sicilies in 1988 and then the return to Erice in 1989, as we actually did: 'For the festival of the Kingdom of the two Sicilies, a Macbeth 'of the two islands': an encounter between Carla Tatò and perhaps one local actor, to melt the mediterranean sound with Shakespeare's unattainable language'.

C. T: After this tour, with this huge and

Figure 4: Arrival of the audience at Incholm Island, 1988.

extraordinary wireless telephone, inside the woods in a green Jaguar, we finally arrived in front of Sweno Castle, with Sweno's grave. There it was impossible to escape the great last speech that our *Macbeth* had with Sweno and therefore from all that history then tells us. We were increasingly fascinated and, you see, the photos say it: there is the Colombaia, then there are Rudi (Fuchs) and Carlo (Quartucci) in Erice, then there is *Sweno* and there is the island of Inchcolm.

In the Catalogue, you have on the left the history of the Kingdom of the two Sicilies and the North, and at this point the images start to merge in parallel, the images of Erice really seem of the island, there is no doubt. Then Segesta arrives and then the Norman Castle and we wondered with Carlo how much Norman and Caesar's influence had reached Scotland. It was beautiful – this encounter to understand peoples and the geography of peoples, a geo-poetics that really interested us a lot, and then put them in relation with each other.

M. B: There is the beautiful page with boats, journeys, travellers, navigators – in parallel, our surveys in Sicily and our surveys in Scotland: 'Marriage between Erice and Inchcolm'.

C. T: A continuous coming and going: from Edinburgh to Inchcolm island, from

Figure 5: Richard Demarco, Inchcolm Island, 1988.

Trapani to Marsala, to the island of Mozia, and to all that incredible journey that was then the Sicily of the Kingdom of the two Sicilies, on the Mediterranean and Inchcolm on the North Sea, and they were absolutely right.

There is a very evocative page in the Catalogue, where we talk about *Opera dei Pupi*. Because *Opera dei Pupi* was represented in Sicily and in the popular tradition in the Kingdom of the two Sicilies, even before *Macbeth*, and we tried to attune these two elements, because we are navigators, we are travellers, the boats and the sea – they exist here and there. This common tradition seemed very beautiful to us: the tradition of the sea. The Catalogue contains the whole beautiful text by Carlo (Quartucci), which explains what this trip to Scotland meant to us: assonances, dissonances, consonances, harmonies and frequencies.

The next image is one of me, in Heinrich von Kleist's *Penthesilea*, attuned to the bloodiest tragedies exactly as in the *Lady* in *Macbeth* and as in Euripides' *Medea*.

Also in the Catalogue, you can see us at work in the courtyard of the Castle, on the left we meet the Director of the Festival Frank Dunlop, and now the images speak for themselves. We began the action from Richard Demarco Gallery, with the three witch girls presenting themselves mute, after which the three young dancers entered a bus guiding the traveller-spectators towards the port where a ferry boat was waiting for us. The bus audience was greeted by Verdi's *Macbeth* and escorted to the port of Edinburgh. We crossed that magnificent iron bridge, accompanied by witches and strange types dressed in a morning dress: musicians playing strange instruments, perched on a stern, on a seat of this ship and of course the travellers were intrigued. And this ferry boat arrived at Inchcolm Island. The arrival was an extraordinary image, because you could see a side of the mountain – I remember it perfectly – on which stood out, sitting in silhouette, the *pipe* players (*pibroch players*), who were wearing half black gloves, because it was freezing cold – in August – and they had to play this pibroch. And there were swarms of white seagulls that reminded me of the entrance of the black crows in Segesta, which had moments like these, especially at sunset, inside the temple of Segesta. At Sweno Castle, when we arrived by ferry boat, there were silhouetted *pibroch* players, I say white doves, but they were actually white seagulls, and there were on the rocks, in the sea, seals that caught something then plunged back in to feed their little ones: an overwhelming image.

The travelling audience arrived and there were two people to welcome them, with two lanterns: one was Carlo Quartucci – the director of that theatrical, sce-

Figure 6: From the left, unkown person, Carlo Quartucci, unkown person, Carla Tatò, Inchcolm Island, 1988.

Figures 7a, b:
From the left,
Juliet Cadzow
and Carla Tatò,
Inchcolm Island,
1988.

nic and performance day – and the other was John Bett, *the porter*. Both without saying a word, Carlo (Quartucci) delivering, as usual, an extraordinary miming performance, of great charm. The porter distributed blankets to all these travellers already cold. During this action our John Bett played the part of the porter and welcomed them as he would have welcomed the King, while (Carlo) Quartucci silently showed them the way to reach the Castle.

M. B: Along the way, there were videos, and almost all the films we mentioned earlier: Carmelo Bene, Akira Kurosawa, Orson Wells, Roman Polanski, and the others.

C. T: Exactly, they were placed on the left of the entrance path to the Castle, with the pibroch players accompanying

Figure 8: John Bett, The Porter, Inchcolm Island, 1988.

them. This at the beginning, while on the way back you went to the other side, on the side of the cliff. And there, on the rocks, in front of the sea, lapped by the waves, there were television-monitors with looped images of *Macbeths* from Vittorio Gassman to Orson Welles, from Toshirō Mifune to Carmelo Bene, all embedded in the rocks; and a tenor and a viola player, perched on the rocks between the televisions and then the audience: these strange travellers wrapped in blankets, who went around and passed in front of Sweno's grave, entered the courtyard and were led into a gallery all arches to then descend into a room where was a large, long black table. Here, they found two mirroring *Ladies*: (Carla) Tatò from Sicily, with a white silk dress, blond hair and signs – evidently – of gold and blood; and our Juliet Cadzow, black, dark-haired, dressed in black silk. And we both went, sometimes together, sometimes now one and now the other, into a series of fragments of *Lady Macbeth*, all fragments that we have chosen as the dramaturgical pathway up to the grand finale. We even recited together "*Tomorrow, and tomor-*

row, and tomorrow", as Macbeth says. And as *Lady*, imagined as the great guide-actress of the whole project, we reiterated how she represented her double image: that of the Kingdom of the two Sicilies, the North and the South, the island of the North Sea and the island of the Magnum southern Mediterranean Sea. We were truly a total emblem of this relationship between different islands, in symbiosis, with the cadence of the beautiful Italian verse, translated from the "blank verse", extraordinary, into an actor's rhythm that created a very exciting, overwhelming situation. I'm recounting it, but perhaps you will remember too. And you never knew when this action ended.

At this point the two *porters*, John Bett and Carlo Quartucci, silently invited the travellers to continue the journey: but the travellers did not want to move. In the end, they moved, except for two, who, given the freedom and emptiness of the room, started taking an immensity of photographs. It was an unusual gesture for us then, and we were tense. We were immobile for a long time and expected to be, but these shots were not expected. We later found out that these photographing visitors were Japanese. In 1988 it was strange, while today it wouldn't be.

The travellers who went in and out of the Castle continuously, found the videos running always accompanied by the tenor and the viola. It was a very evocative "video installation". Televisions, monitors, TV sets resting on the rocks of the cliff on which Inchcolm Castle stands, along the path of the travellers, but practically on the sea, lapped by the lively waves of the North Sea; running and each showing different looped sequences from the most relevant films and musical works made on Macbeth. And little by little they were found immersed in water because the rising tide was submerging the monitors too.

M. B: In fact, I don't know how we managed not to spoil them.

C. T: I don't know why they still worked, yet they were violently lapped by the water, it was very beautiful.

M. B: You know, in my opinion the pibroch players actually welcomed us on the island, because in the Catalogue I see the three brass players (trumpet, trombone and tuba), who in my opinion were on the bus, while the pibroch players welcomed us on the island and then climbed to the top of the Castle tower and stayed with us until the end.

C. T: It is absolutely so: the players were the brass.

M. B: And there were Richard (Demarco) and Jane, his partner, who acted as narrators along the way to the island and delivered the travellers to the two *porters* on the island.

C. T: On their return, the pibroch players were frozen to death too, but they lasted long enough to farewell the spectators-travellers, who were returning by ferry boat. We, on the other hand, had boats waiting for us and welcoming us, actors and pibroch players together. The cold immediately led them to drink from the flasks they had with them of twenty-year-old Scotch whiskey in large gulps. I, who did not drink, "drained" this extraordinary malt whiskey from the pibroch players. Carlo (Quartucci), on the other hand, enjoyed it at full blast: and drinking and singing we all returned to the port in friendship. A great adventure.

M. B: Scrolling through the diary, I find that we made a survey trip in July, while obviously this event happened in August, around August 15th, in a terrifying cold. I also found a letter from Richard (Demarco), dated June 6, waiting for us to introduce the pibroch performers, Juliet (Cadzow) and Bill Paterson, who was supposed to play *Macbeth*, but gave up and was replaced by John (Bett) as *porter* instead of as *Macbeth*.

Then there is this question of the "film" of which I find a note in the diary.

C. T: *Channel 4*, the TV network, wanted to shoot a documentary on the Festival, and on this Macbethian event in particular: I remember that there were two important arrivals during that period, which was a bit of rehearsal for us, to understand the space and understand which "pieces" of Macbeth to choose. Do you remember that Franca Rame came to see us?

M. B: I don't remember of Franca Rame; I remember instead that we went to see Sean Connery, who was in his castle waiting for the award of an *Honoris Causa* Degree in I don't remember which University lost in the middle of nowhere.

C. T: Nowhere, in fact, but immersed in the greenery of the surrounding countryside. And when we told Sean (Connery) that we were on Inchcolm's island and we were playing *Macbeth*, like a madman and like all actors, he began to repeat: '*We don't say "Macbeth", we only say "the Scottish Tragedy"*'. It was terrible bad luck! But we also said, with Ferruccio Marotti: 'He repeated it too many times,

Figure 9: From left Carlo Quartucci and Carla Tatò, Meikle Seggie, 1988

Figure 10: Macbeth by La Zattera di Babele in the programme/brochure, RDG Edinburgh Festival 1989 programme of exhibitions and theatre. The performances were cancelled.

he brought us bad luck!'. And after Sean Connery, we did not pronounce this couplet anymore.

M. B: This film then didn't happen, right?

C. T: No, even if Demarco kept talking about it. And again in 1989 when he came to Erice.

M. B: I also found a note from (Richard) Demarco: "*Call sheet!*" of 8 July 1988 relating to a meeting with the crew, the

MACBETH   LA ZATTERA DI BABELE

An Official Festival Production

After last year's experiment with a Prologue to Macbeth on the Island of Inchcolm in the Firth of Forth, this Rome and Sicily based company return to present their version of the play on the site where Macbeth accepted the surrender of the Norwegian king and which was a holy place associated with Scottish royalty until the 16th century. A highly original and apposite venue for a new look at "the Scottish play".

Regular bus and train services connect Edinburgh with South Queensferry from which the ferry to Inchcolm departs 7pm, returning at 9pm.

NB. Tickets are only available through the Official Festival Box Office. Tel 031 225 5756

INCHCOLM ISLAND (Ferry leaves 7pm) 14-17 Aug and 20-22 Aug £15

producer, the director, the cameramen, Demarco Gallery: but it stopped there. The cast would have been: Richard Demarco, Sandy Moffat, Sean Connery, Carla Tatò, Carlo Quartucci and Marina Bistolfi; good company!

C. T: It was the company that (Richard) Demarco had chosen with Channel 4 and he was proud of it; even the director of the festival, Frank Dunlop, knew about this. And I believe that Franca Rame, who was there on a visit for other things, also had news of this project: she had come to meet and greet us and to hear what we were doing. The project, however, was put on hold.

M. B: It was put on hold, even if something could have been shot that day, because I find written in the diary 'set up' at the Demarco Gallery, and then to go to the University of Saint Andrews, about the '*Film with Connery in grounds of University*': but I don't think we made it.

C. T: I don't know this, only Demarco can know. I know that I have seen the images. Apart from that, we were there, and Richard (Demarco) organized this production as a surprise, with us unaware, saying the unspeakable word, but then we witnessed something. I saw Carlo (Quartucci) and Sean (Connery) next to each other, and we all said to each other: 'But he's shorter than Carlo (Quartucci), Sean (Connery)!', who appears very tall and looked like him, it's true. Although Sean had finer, gentler features, while Carlo had a stronger stance.

M. B: Connery wore a robe, I remember it when we went to visit him at his castle: he wore it with a long *Honoris Causa* degree tunic and he came from the set of *The Name of the Rose*, so he had a beard.

C. T: However, they were very handsome, I must say! And having both of them next to me made a huge impression on me.

M. B: So this film was never made, perhaps due to production or budget problems.

C. T: I don't know, we should ask (Richard) Demarco.

(*Thanks to Anna Maria Cesareo for her collaboration.*)

IN MEMORIAM: Marco Maria Gazzano
died 7 June 2022

Prof. Marco Maria Gazzano was a world renowned expert in film and pioneer of electronic arts and intermediality theory.

From the beginning of his career, Prof. Gazzano fostered the experimentation of video and digital art and championed the work of pioneers of experimental visual art, film, music and theatre.

He had a powerful and strong activist spirit and a vision of how culture and art could influence politics, society and, ultimately, life.

We were honoured to be able to call Prof. Gazzano a friend. He supported the REWIND projects and was truly generous with his time and precious materials. His books and his lectures constitute a fundamental grounding for our investigations, and it is our hope they will continue to inspire and influence future generations of scholars, theoreticians, historians, artists, curators, and practitioners.

Our long conversations informed key decisions and enlightened new paths in research.

Prof. Gazzano will be dearly missed, but we are honoured with the task of continuing his legacy.

7

Demarco and Yugoslavia in the 1970s

Jon Blackwood

During the Cold War period, relations between the UK and Yugoslavia were couched entirely in the frames of politics, economics or military history; in the later years of socialist Yugoslavia, from the later seventies onwards, links were also developed through state-run tourism, and the international components of youth work brigades, who helped to complete major infrastructure projects. Art was little considered, in the context of the UK, much less so than it had been during the period of Royal Yugoslavia (1918–41), when the Croatian sculptor Ivan Meštrović (1883–1962) developed a significant international following from the period of the First World War, through to the middle 1930s. Following the end of the second world war, very little was known in the UK of contemporary art in Yugoslavia from the late 1940s through to the early 1970s.

The fluctuating contours of the cultural relationship between the UK and Yugoslavia are perhaps for another essay, however. In this text we will focus on the pioneering nine-day trip taken by Richard Demarco to Yugoslavia in December 1972, and its consequences not only for the international profile of Yugoslav art, but also for relations between Yugoslav artists and cultural ecologies in neighbouring countries. The details of Demarco's nine-day trip, organized by the Yugoslav Federal Institute of Culture, Education & Science, can be found in a fascinating typewritten account in the Demarco Archive. Reflecting on what seems to have been an exhausting itinerary, Demarco reflected that:

> I realized I had merely scratched the surface of the art world in Yugoslavia, though I had been on four all night journeys by train, one jet flight, and I had visited five cities in nine days, and had been in twenty studios and met fifty-one artists, and twenty-five art critics and gallery directors ... .[1]

In order for us to understand the impact that this initial exhaustive trip would have had, it is firstly necessary to try and chart the cultural geography of Yugoslavia in the early 1970s, and the relationship between the Yugoslav art world and the rest of Europe.

Ever since the *Informbiro* period of 1948, when Yugoslavia had been expelled from the COMINFORM group of socialist countries, the country's leader, Josip Broz Tito, had sought to differentiate his country's politics and culture from elsewhere in the Communist world.[2] Economically, this meant a Yugoslav variant of Marxism described as 'self-managed socialism', whereas, in terms of visual culture, what came to be known as "socialist aestheticism" was hegemonic, from the mid 1950s.

The break with Stalinist orthodoxy had three important consequences for the development of post-war Yugoslav art. Firstly, Yugoslav citizens had unprecedented access to touring exhibitions of Western art in the 1950s. In 1952, a survey exhibition of the latest trends in French art toured Belgrade, Skopje, Zagreb and Ljubljana; the following year, a contemporary Dutch exhibition, including a representative sample of the work of De Stijl, toured the same cities with the exception of Ljubljana. The canonical exhibition, however, in the development of Yugoslav art, and reflecting the unique profile that the country enjoyed in post war geopolitics, was the 1956 show 'Contemporary Art of the USA' which included all the prominent Abstract Expressionist painters. It will be apparent, then, that whilst Yugoslavia developed its own kind of Communist government, culturally it was just as interested in developments in the capitalist world.

Yugoslavia's independence from the Soviet model of Communist development, after 1948, also sealed the fate of a budding Yugoslav 'socialist realism'. This style, focusing on the achievements of the working class, and the leading role played in society by the Communist Party, was hegemonic in art academies and teaching institutions elsewhere in Eastern Europe. By contrast, as Miško Šuvaković and others have shown, 'socialist aestheticism' emerged in painting and sculpture in the 50s and 60s, as a form of modernist response to the ideological strictures of socialist realism. This particular form has been described as: '... aestheticized, nondogmatic, ideologically neutral, and artistically independent expression and presentation'.[3]

The third consequence follows on

logically. In Yugoslavia, Modernism was not a subversive or counter-revolutionary force, but instead was stripped of its ideological content, and its practice fully sanctioned by the cultural and political authorities. As a result, a pleasant, unchallenging, formally modernist series of paintings and sculptures gained official recognition as the 1960s developed, which eschewed politics in return for official tolerance. Examples of such work can be found across Yugoslavia's successor republics, and the contemporary cultural response to this legacy is mixed, to say the least.

In response, younger artists turned away from this 'official' modernism as encouraged by the cultural authorities, and began in a variety of ways to explore new media and new possibilities for self-expression.

It is also critical to keep in mind that there was never any such thing as 'Yugoslav' art, or a recognisable 'Yugoslav' style, either during the period we are considering here. With this in mind, each challenge to socialist aestheticism took on distinctly local flavours, in each republican capital.[4] Groups such as the Slovenian *reist*, process art group OHO in Kralj and Ljubljana, contributed alongside the emergent conceptualists, performance artists and video artists, of the newly established Students Cultural Centre (SKC) in Belgrade, whilst, in Zagreb, the series of 'New Tendencies exhibitions' that ran from 1961–1973, showing the work of *informel* grouping 'Gorgona' and, later, the conceptual interventions of artists such as Goran Trbuljak and Braco Dimitirijević, added a further layer to the complex set of interrelationships and local differentiation that made up the practice of contemporary art across Yugoslavia. These differing manifestations of conceptualism, anti-art, anti- modernism, performance and installation began to be understood in Yugoslavia at the beginning of the 1970s as 'New Art Practice'. The critic Bojana Pejić summarises the implications ably:

> The New Art Practice was a *constellation* which inserted itself into the 'body' of Yugoslav communist society and involved, at first, artists from Novi Sad, Ljubljana, Zagreb, Belgrade, and later Sarajevo, as well as art critics and museum and gallery curators belonging to the younger generation. The major characteristic of the New Art Practice was its contentious consciousness, which was otherwise central to the cultural climate after 1968.[5]

The emergence of the New Art Practice(s), ultimately, led to a subtle differentiation in Yugoslav cultural policy as the 1970s developed. The various artists and 'scenes' associated with new conceptual strategies, with video and performance, tended to be given a great deal of international prominence – with Demarco's two Edinburgh exhibitions in 1973 (Figure 1) and 1975 forming part of that overall international presentation. Domestically, however, major state-owned exhibiting spaces, with access controlled through local artists' unions, tended to favour more those artists whose work in painting, sculpture and graphics had a bigger audience and accorded more with the political self-perception of the Yugoslav space. Painters such as Lazar Vujaklija, or sculptors such as Antun Augustinićić and Dušan Džamonja tended to have a much bigger following with local audiences.

Demarco's first encounter, then, with the Yugoslav art world, came just as the first challenges to the orthodoxies of socialist aestheticism were gaining traction. Two centres of activity were critical in providing a space for this new alternative to develop; firstly, the series of international theatre exhibitions in Belgrade,

known as BITEF, from 1968 onwards, and also the newly commissioned Students' Cultural Centre in Belgrade, where many of the 'New Art Practice' figures were based early in their career, and which acted as a central node of ideas and cultural exchange, for other counterhegemonic art scenes around the Federation.

The freelance curator and critic, Biljana Tomić, organised the visual components of the BITEF exhibitions. In addition to providing exposure for emergent conceptual artists in Yugoslavia, such as "OHO", she also invited significant European practitioners to Belgrade, amongst them Jannis Kounellis, and Michelangelo Pistoletto. Tomić also intervened at the SKC, alongside Dunja Blažević, in programming a series of performance art festivals called *April Meeting: Extended Media* that lasted from 1972–77, with Gina Pane, John Baldessari, and Joseph Beuys amongst the artists to visit Belgrade in that period. The effect of the BITEF and SKC programmes was to give international exposure to the new developments in art in Yugoslavia, whilst providing homegrown artists with exposure and contacts in a fast- developing European conceptual and performance scene.

Demarco did visit the SKC on his first day in Belgrade, on 5 December 1972,

Figure 1: *Rhythm 10*, performance by Marina Abramović for the RDG at Melville College, Edinburgh. Eight Yugoslav Artists, 19 August 1973. Edinburgh Arts 1973.

where he encountered Biljana Tomić, Raša Todosijević and Zoran Popović, amongst others. In his report, he noted that these two artists '... seemed to make a team and were not afraid to experiment most courageously in film and into activities which questioned the nature of exhibitions'.[6] He also noted the role that the SKC had played in introducing Beuys to Belgrade audiences.

However, it would be wrong to see this first trip to Yugoslavia as focusing only on the 'New Art Practices'. Demarco's itinerary, drawn up by Yugoslav officials, saw him encountering a remarkable cross section of artists and curators, from the painter and mosaicist Gligor Ćemerski in Skopje, to Radoslav Putar and the Croatian naïve artist Ivan Laćković in Zagreb. Demarco also spent time in Sarajevo, where he met Curator of the Art Gallery of Bosnia-Herzegovina, Azra Begić, and Ljubljana, where he was photographed in the studio of the Dragans.

In all, he was exposed to the full spectrum of art practice across differing centres in the country, from socialist aestheticism, through naïve art, large-scale public sculpture, and emergent conceptual, performance and video practices. He also noted, with approval, the practice of allocating the top floor of any newly built tower block for space as artist's studios and apartments, which he had encountered both in New Belgrade and Skopje.

A good example of the myriad impressions the Scots-Italian cultural broker must have had of visual culture in Yugoslavia can be found in a photograph in the Demarco archive. The architect Iskra Grabul (Figure 2) is shown in her studio alongside a maquette for the extraordinary *Makedonium* building, subsequently erected at Kruševo in south Macedonia by August 1974. This was an outworking of a drawing and discussion process that had probably begun in late 1971, between the artists and architects involved in the building; Iskra, her husband, the architect Jordan Grabul, the monumental fresco painter Borko Lazeski, who was responsible for the building's stained glass, and Petar Mazev, who designed biomorphic sculpted reliefs for the interior. As the canonical MOMA exhibition *Towards a Concrete Utopia* of 2018–19 demonstrated, Yugoslavia's cultural actors had an extraordinary freedom in opening up both the built environment and range of monumental sculpture in Yugoslavia, from the middle 1960s until the early 1980s – remarkably inventive and daring three dimensional forms that deserve much better treatment than their contemporary de-politicised & exoticised presentation in Western photo books and projects.

For all the remarkable diversity of this first foray into unfamiliar cultural milieus, Demarco's opening exhibition back in Edinburgh, *Eight Yugoslav Artists*, in August 1973, was based entirely on the New Art Practices' that he had seen on the first day of his trip, at the SKC in Belgrade. A document in the Demarco archive, dated 28 December 1972, shows an initial proposal for an exhibition of seventy artists from six different urban centres, that was submitted for consideration to the Yugoslav Federal Institute; presumably, the sheer logistical and travel implications of this early proposal, and subsequent negotiation, saw this ambitious idea whittled down to a much more coherent grouping of mainly Belgrade artists.[7] Of the eight chosen to be shown at Melville College in August 1973, only Ljubljana's Nuša and Srećo Dragan were based elsewhere. Radomir Damnjanović-Damnjan was by that time living in Milan, and Gergelj 'Gera' Urkom

Figure 2: Iskra Grabul, co-designer with Jordan Grabul of the Ilinden Monument, Krushevo, Macedonia, with a maquette of the monument in her studio in Belgrade, Serbia (then Yugoslavia), December 1972. Photographed by Richard Demarco during a visit to Yugoslavia in preparation for the exhibition *Eight Yugoslav Artists*, at the RDG in August–September 1973.

in London, but both these artists had deep roots in Belgrade's contemporary art scene.

However, all of the selected artists in the first Edinburgh show had worked together closely in an intense period of collaboration and exhibition from summer 1972 onwards. The art writer and historian Jasna Tijardović chronicled the significance of the exhibitions BITEF 6, in September 1972, and 'October '72' at SKC in Belgrade; Demarco's visit coincided with this latter show's end, and a hybrid of it mutated into the *Eight Yugoslav Artists* show of August 1973.

The evening featured the debut performance of Abramović's iconic *Rhythm 10*, with ten knives. This is a piece in which the artist plays the Russian game of "five-finger- fillet". She rhythmically stabs the space between the fingers of her splayed hand, accidentally cutting herself in the process. Every time she stabs herself, the knife changes, until all ten have been used. The artist then listens to a recording of the first round of ten knives, and attempts to repeat the injuries inflicted on herself, so that, in her

own words, 'the mistakes of time past and time present can be synchronized'.[8]

Paripović, Popović, Todosijević and Gergelj Urkom performed simultaneously alongside Abramović, with Urkom giving a version of his performance piece *Upholstering a Chair*. The documentary photographs show Joseph Beuys amongst an attentive and interested audience. The simultaneity of the performance would have left a very powerful impression of the closeness of these artists, their temporary suppression of individual identity in a group endeavour, and their navigation of different routes of physical privation and practical humour, in a constant and urgent interrogative development.

The Edinburgh show was also significant for the first showing of the work of Nuša & Srećo Dragan outside of the Yugoslav context. The duo had produced the first video work in the Yugoslav context, *Belo mleko Belih prsi* [White Milk of White Breasts], which appeared in 1969. In actual fact, this work is a still image of a woman's breast, with a bead of milk visible; playing across this image is a sequence of changing, edited graphic signs. This video piece stands at a turning point, between the traditional still image, and the coming new techniques of editing, cutting and mixing. Nuša had worked at the British Film Institute in London for a period in 1972 where her knowledge of video and television techniques grew exponentially. The piece shown in Edinburgh in 1973, *Project Communication of Gastronomy*, was a mix of still photography, film and happening-style experience, an assured and striking synthesis of contemporary forms and ideas.

Following the conclusion of the 1973 exhibition, Demarco's mind turned towards the realization of the much more ambitious, broadly based exhibition, which he had first suggested to the Federal Institute of Culture in December 1972. He was to return to Yugoslavia regularly in the next three years, meeting up with Marina Abramović and Raša Todosijević during a visit to various studios in Zagreb and Belgrade in 1974; he was back for a brief meeting with both these artists at Motovun in Istria, in the Summer of 1975, during an Edinburgh Arts tour.

Motovun, as Laura Leuzzi, and Branka Benčić have shown in different essays,[9] was a key location for cross-fertilisation of emergent video art form and production between Italy and Yugoslavia. The link between Motovun and Demarco's work can perhaps be found most directly in the early work of Sanja Iveković, who was able to have some of her work produced in the Italian context, bypassing the limitations of Yugoslav conditions for production.

A good example of Iveković's 1970s work is *Make Up Make Down*, a nine-minute video made first in black and white in 1976, produced by Galleria del Cavallino in Italy, and later transferred to colour in 1978. The subject of the work is the private, intimate moment of applying make-up. The artist is not visible in the film, but the focus is rather on the make-up products, and how Iveković interacts with them during the process. The work speaks to a broader narrative of the commodification of identity and desire, and through a pitiless examination of those processes, inviting broader analysis of the rituals that women engage in before presenting a public persona.

By the time Iveković was showing this work at Motovun in 1976, the touring run of the exhibition of the remarkable *ASPECT '75* exhibition was well under way. Whereas *Eight Yugoslav Artists* had only managed to give a brief snapshot of one contemporary art scene in Belgrade, *ASPECT '75*, in every sense, gave as full a picture as was possible then of art practice in Yugoslavia, from Croatian naïve painting and 'socialist aestheticism' through to performance and video. Forty-eight artists participated, whilst the range of introductory essays reads almost as a who's who of significant Yugoslav curators of the mid 1970s. This is still a well-remembered generation of colleagues one of whom, Marijan Susovski (Figure 3), then Director of the Gallery of Contemporary Art in Zagreb, was significant in developing links between Yugoslav video artists and their counterparts in Austria and Italy in the middle 1970s, as well as encouraging the developing career of Braco Dimitrijević. In his essay, director of the Galleries of the City of Zagreb, Radoslav Putar, makes direct reference to the video work of Ivekovicì and the ideas of Dimitrijević and Goran Trbuljak; the Ljubljana critic Aleksander Bassin discusses the video work of the Dragans, and it's complicated emergence from the milieu of the Slovenian *avant-garde* in the late 1960s.

The catalogue, featuring a blown-up image of a Yugoslav passport with its iconic coat of arms in gold, still stands today, thirty-five years later, as one of the few informative sources in English on experimental Yugoslav art in the post war period. When the exhibition opened at Edinburgh's Fruitmarket Gallery in August 1975, it was quickly clear that this was a profound and carefully chosen survey of art in Yugoslavia, which well reflected Demarco's lively and sensitive awareness of the differing artistic scenes and how they worked (or didn't work) together. His surveying of the Yugoslav art world, which reached far beyond the central Ljubljana–Zagreb–Belgrade axis, was a near unique phenomenon amongst Western curators and art historians at this period. Other than the major survey exhibition, "4,000 years of Yugoslav art" held in Paris in 1971, no other exhibition in Western Europe matched the ambition of the Edinburgh exhibition during this decade. Further, it was the only significant survey exhibition of Yugoslav art in the UK during the entire existence of the federation (1918–91).

ASPECT '75, which toured after the closure of the Fruitmarket show to five other venues in 1975–76,[10] proved to be a survey of an art world on the point of changing profoundly, again. Looking through some of the exhibitors' biographies in the catalogue, we see that Gergelj Urkom had left Belgrade for London; Braco Dimitrijević was on the point of leaving Zagreb behind; and, by the time that the tour had finished, Marina Abramović had left Belgrade for Amsterdam, stating that it was becoming increasingly difficult to make the kind of work that she wanted to make in the Yugoslav context. Of the Belgrade grouping, only Todosijević continued a focus on performance and body art, whilst Paripović spent the second half of the decade experimenting with video art, encouraged by the pioneering work of Dunja Blažević, as head

of programming at SKC in Belgrade (1976–81) and later as the initiator of "TV Gallery" on Yugoslav Television from 1981 onwards. Other artists who took part in the show – most notably Sanja Iveković – was later to come to the attention of the Yugoslav authorities for the content of her work.[11]

In our days, even with the new and unpleasant realities of travel during Covid times, international travel for artists and curators, pursuing opportunities and installing shows, is taken for granted. Fifty years ago, during Demarco's first visit to Yugoslavia, such itineraries were very rare, and his journey around Yugoslavia and subsequent building and enhancing relationships made there, were nothing short of unique. Demarco's work in making links not only between Yugoslavia and the UK in terms of contemporary art, as well as his (indirect) role in helping to grow connections between Yugoslav contemporary artists, galleries and producers in Italy, were to leave a significant mark.

Demarco is also one of the few remaining links to an extremely lively transEuropean set of artistic exchanges; sadly, of the generation of directors and critics who contributed to his *ASPECT '75* catalogue, only the Serbian critic Ješa Denegri remains alive.

It is best perhaps to finish with a

Figure 3: Marijan Susovski and Marina Abramović in Abramović's studio, Belgrade, Serbia (then Yugoslavia), showing documentation of her performance *Rhythm 10*, 1974. Photographed during a visit to Yugoslavia in preparation for *Aspects '75* (49 Yugoslavian artists, shown at the Fruitmarket Gallery, Edinburgh, 29 September – 25 October 1975).

short anecdote. When I was curating an exhibition of contemporary art from Macedonia at Summerhall in Edinburgh in October 2017 (Figure 4), our guests from Skopje were perhaps most delighted by meeting Richard Demarco at an afternoon seminar to discuss the themes of the show. Many of his memories of Skopje in December 1972 – of the newly commissioned Museum of Contemporary Art, of the old exhibiting (and still active) spaces at Daut Pasha Hamam, which he visited, mapped on carefully to the experiences and lived realities of this generation of artists whose careers developed long after his visit. The touching continuity between the impresario's memories and the experiences of successive generations of artists is, I believe, very rare to find, and speaks of a legacy of enormous significance.

Figure 4: Richard Demarco visiting Macedonians at Summerhall on 7 October 2017. [Photo courtesy Jon Blackwood.]

Endnotes

1. 'Richard Demarco's Report on his visit to Yugoslavia', unpublished typescript, Demarco Archive. http://www.demarco-archive.ac.uk
2. 'Informbiro' is the term used to describe the period 1948–55 in Yugoslav history, when the country broke with the Soviet Union and stood apart from the Communist world, in addition to enjoying a strengthening of relations with Western Europe, and the United States. The Informbiro period came to an end with the signing of a joint declaration in Belgrade, by Tito and Khrushchev, in June 1955. Formally, however, Yugoslavia remained aloof from Eastern bloc political formations such as the Warsaw Pact and the COMECON.
3. Miško Šuvaković, 'Impossible Histories', in Dubravka Djurić and Miško Šuvaković (eds.), *Impossible Histories: Historical Avant-Gardes, Neo-Avant Gardes, and Post Avant-Gardes in Yugoslavia, 1918–91* (Cambridge, Mass. & London: MIT Press, 2003), p. 10.
4. In the Communist period, from 1945, Yugoslavia was officially a federation of six socialist republics – Slovenia (Ljubljana), Croatia (Zagreb), Bosnia-Hercegovina (Sarajevo), Montenegro (Titograd), Serbia (Belgrade, also the federal capital) and Macedonia (Skopje), and two autonomous regions, Kosovo (Pristina) and Vojvodina (Novi Sad). Each republic and autonomous region had a local art scene based in their capital city, although at the time of Demarco's visit, it was thought that Ljubljana, Zagreb and Belgrade were the main centres of interest. Seen in this context, his decision to also visit Skopje and Sarajevo, and express disappointment at lacking the time to visit Novi Sad, shows a real ambition to challenge the received view of art in Yugoslavia.
5. Bojana Pejić, 'Body based Art: Serbia and Montenegro' in *Body and East from the 1960s to the Present* (Ljubljana: Moderna Galerija, 1998).
6. Richard Demarco, *op. cit.*, p. 2.
7. Demarco initially requested that artists from Ljubljana, Zagreb, Belgrade, Sarajevo, Skopje, and Novi Sad, submit work for exhibition in Edinburgh, with an unspecified number of the seventy names travelling. Such a proposal was clearly unrealistic given that only eight months were available between Demarco's trip to Yugoslavia, and the opening of the exhibition in August 1973. The final list of exhibitors was: Marina Abramović, Radomir Damnjan, Nuša & Sreco Dragan, Nesa Paripović, Zoran Popović, Rasa Todosijević and Gergely Urkom.

8. Marina Abramović, *The Artist Body* (Milan: Edizioni Charta, 1998) p. 56. A fragment of a 1999 performance of *Rhythm 10* can be seen online at: http://www.youtube.com/watch?v=h9-HVwEbdCo

9. See Leuzzi, L (2018), "The Fourth Motovun Encounter A Platform for Artistic Experimentation", accessible here: https://amp.issuu.com/fundacjaarton1/docs/arton_book_revisiting_heritage_-_pd/84, and Benčić, Branka (2016), "Motovun Meeting 1976 : The First Video Art Workship in Croatia", CINEMANIAC 2016, Pula. Accessible here: cinemaniac-thinkfilm.com/wp-content/uploads/2015/07/booklet_essay.pdf

10. These were: Municipal Gallery of Modern Art, Dublin, November-December 1975; Turnpike Gallery, Leigh, January–February 1976; Ulster Museum, Belfast, March–April 1976; University of Sussex, April–May 1976, the tour finishing with an exhibition at the Third Eye Centre in Glasgow.

11. Iveković, notoriously, did a performance entitled *Triangle* in 1979, when she simulated masturbation on the balcony of her Zagreb flat, as President Tito's official limousine and honour guard passed by on the road below. The performance was broken up by the authorities.

Appendix 1

Travelling with Richard Demarco

Gabriella Cardazzo

I have been asked several times to write my thoughts about Richard Demarco, but I have done so only rarely. Not because there aren't things to say about him. On the contrary, it is because there would be so many things to say about him that I almost never manage to gather up my thoughts into a text of acceptable length.

The principal reason for my hesitation is: I am asked to speak about Richard Demarco, a person completely outside the so-called concept of "normal", a person who is controversial and innocent, but at times as complex as his origins, suspended between the British and Mediterranean cultures, and different religions.

When we speak of Richard, of his life and work, it is clear that we enter into an unpredictable place which has very little to do with the conventional. But, at the same time, I am fascinated by his world because it allows me to explore new dimensions and forms of freedom which, in the end, are essential to my own personal quest.

A trip with Richard is an event that can last years: from one's youth to the autumn of one's life. It is difficult for me now to map it out, but I know it happened. And, at a certain moment of my life, I

Figure 1: From left to right, unknown passer-by, William MacLellan, Gabriella Cardazzo, and Guido Sartorelli, in Edinburgh, 23–24 August 1975. [Photo by Mario 'Piccolo' Sillani Djerrahian.]

this road or not? In Richard's words, art came into my life with diverse words and images, and it created new forms. Art expanded in the ether and rendered me a participant in the significance of my existence, more conscious of the new rôle not only of my work but, above all, of the relationships I would share with others.

From that day, the landscape around me changed, but the intensity of travel as a quest continued: Berkeley Pier in San Francisco, or walking along the winding road of Meikle Seggie in Scotland, the solstice in Malta at Hagar Qim, or summer afternoons exploring Sardegna's nuragic sites ... .

During trips with Richard, there is never truly enough time to reflect: everything is experienced, surpassed, and re-proposed again in a different way an hour later, and to which we have to adapt and rewrite the original story.

The speed of all that happens makes it such that the landscapes and the humans that inhabit it interact in an infinite vortex ... different voices, faces, languages and cultures. There are no more boundaries because Richard's uni-

Figure 2: Gabriella Cardazzo and American artist Joseph Reeder at the Galleria del Cavallino, Venice, 9–21 July 1977. Edinburgh Arts 1977.

decided to board that moving train from which I have perhaps never disembarked.

From the highway we could see the towers of San Gimignano and the question came up: should I continue along

Figure 3: From left to right, Wieslaw Borowski, Tadeusz Kantor, Zbigniew Gostomski (background), Martita Hyams, Gabriella Cardazzo, Anselmo Anselmi at the Edinburgh College of Art during Kantor's Cricot 2 Theatre production of *The Dead Class*, August/September 1976.

Figure 4: Paolo and Gabriella Cardazzo in their office at Galleria del Cavallino during the exhibition *John Knox, Iain Patterson, Ainslie Yule*, organised in collaboration with the RDG, 26 September – 25 October 1974..

verse does not have borders, just as there aren't any between art and life.

Consequently, after those memorable trips, the return home was always melancholic… everything around me was "normal" and calm. The world became the objects that surrounded me, and the turbulence and madness of the trip was substituted by deafening silence.

What is Richard — and what we are all – searching for during our lifetime? Suspended between calm and madness one realises that it is *art*: it has its own space and its great *raison d'être*.

Richard's role is that of an initiator who brought me onto a road that in my youth I had never thought of undertaking. Between light and shadow, he was a benchmark, his determination bringing me closer to the *credo* for which he has always fought, for which he has fallen and then picked himself up again.

As for the rest — the exhibitions, the galleries, the celebrity – that surrounds that world is less important. The life and the work of an artist proliferates in its own world: the world of the soul and of the great quest to find a light in the mystery of human beings.

October 2020

Appendix 2

La Strada, Le Route, The Road
an exhibition about the life of Richard Demarco

Deirdre MacKenna

La Strada, Le Route, The Road was an exhibition about the life of Richard Demarco Initiated and produced by Deirdre MacKenna for Museo Nazionale del Molise, Castello Pandone, Venafro, Italy. 12 October 2019 to 12 January 2020

Figure 1: Drawing of Carmino Demarco by Richard Demarco 1946. [Courtesy of the Demarco Archive.]

This exhibition *La Strada, Le Route, The Road* was one element of a wider research-led programme I devised to enable an international diasporic community to reflect on the transition of its identity.

Richard Demarco would be the first member of the diaspora to be presented in the 'home' location, offering an opportunity to reflect on experiences which punctuate gradual change over multiple generations of time, and the identity of the diasporic community 'abroad'.

Richard Demarco has been an influential figure in my life for over thirty years: like his, my heritage is populated by ancestors who originated in the mountain villages surrounding Venafro, and I share the practice of researching, commissioning, producing and presenting narratives through visual art in an ongoing process piecing together fractured stories.

I presentrd Richard's work in Venafro as it is an anchor town in the international diasporic community that we are members of; set on the eastern limit of the flat Casalina plain which links Naples with Rome, it is a strategic cultural and commercial junction before the ascent into the Mainarde mountains which block east from west central Italy. Human travel is etched into the topography surrounding Venafro, in the *'tratturi'* (mile-wide roadways visible only in satellite images which evidence thousands of years of seasonal nomadism), in the pilgrimage routes exiting Europe towards the Holy Land, and in the empty rural villages, for centuries over-populated but now quietly crumbling into the forest.

The current flow of migration from Venafro's communities started in the 1830s, and this apparently sleepy rural community has become the central cog in its diasporic community located in capital cities throughout Europe, Russia, Australia, the USA, Canada and Brazil.

The complex sense of identity at the heart of the Venafro diaspora is compounded in many ways, not least by the failure of successive public administrations to acknowledge its citizens-abroad and provide means for collective self-reflection; with the opening of Museo Nazionale del Molise, Castello Pandone in December 2014 the possibility arrived for members of the diasporic community to engage in an open process of finding itself. *La Strada, Le Route, The Road* was part of the programme I had devised and already presented in some of these cities, and was the third exhibition I devised for Castello Pandone; predecing exhibitions introduced some of the causal factors of outward migration of agrarian workers such as steady employment op-

Figure 2: Drawing of Mr Mancini by Richard Demarco, probably1948. [Courtesy of Cultural Documents.]

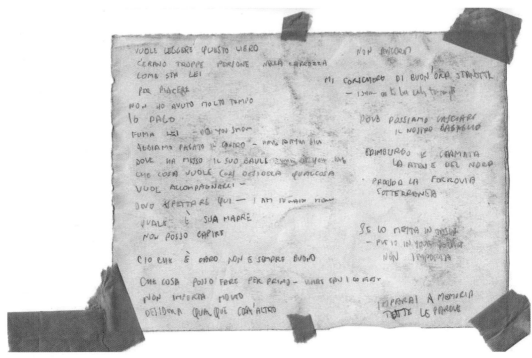

Figure 3:
Italian–English
Notes by Richard
Demarco 1948.

portunities provided by the development of railways from Naples in the 1840s and the occupation of the territory as a site of sustained WWII conflict during the 1940s.

I researched the exhibition content during a series of meetings with Richard Demarco and Charles Stephens in 2017 and 2018 and identified the images in three ways: from the archives at Summerhall, by asking Richard to search further through his own personal archives, and by approaching some of his family members. Previously unpublished images include, amongst others, a self-portrait made by Richard aged eighteen, his drawings of his father Carmino, drawings of the Mancini family models who are part of the same diaspora which Richard made while a student at ECA, and images from his lesson-plan sketches as a young teacher, which illustrate him thinking through the roadway as a metaphor.

The images were arranged in vitrines in chronological order, from ancestry to today; I worked with museum staff to ensure that attenders entered the three galleries at the beginning of the exhibition-route and completed their journey in the Gran Sala, with views over Venafro and the Casalina plain below, which offer escape from the rural, agrarian way of life along routes towards cities beyond the horizon.

Rather than describe my view of how the exhibition was relevant to the community members of the Venafro area, posters announcing Richard's surname (indigenous to the community) activated an open enquiry process "qui è / who is he?", and a booklet in English and Italian languages provided information about each of the images.

The first vitrine contained Richard's family tree alongside photographs of ancestral events set in an increasingly diverse range of international locations, portraying each successive generation's location in an ever more distant city, with the spectre of war constantly present in the background of Richard's own forma-

Figure 4: Richard Demarco pointing to Val Comino October 2019. [Courtesy of Cultural Documents.]

Figure 5: Richard Demarco with his drawing of Mr Mancini, 2017. [Courtesy of Cultural Documents.]

tive years. I knew that Richard's images would resonate strongly with images in the viewer's personal family archives and that in recognising chapters of Demarco's life, I anticipated that they would self-identify with Richard and start to process their encounter through the exhibition simultaneously through their own ancestry and sense of their own international diasporic self.

The second vitrine contained images of Richard's youth including his self-portrait, his drawings of his father, and the Mancini family models, linking Richard back into the nineteenth century European Belle Epoque; when they arrived in new cities, the creative and entrepreneurial ancestors of this diaspora contributed to dynamic cultural advances in many ways such as by importing and marketing goods as exotic new products and working as models to avant-garde artists including Matisse and Modigliani, evident today in museums throughout Europe, in the sculptures of Hyde Park and Place de la Concorde, and in 'La Semeuse', the iconic image on the French franc.

The images in the second room continued Demarco's early artistic works; sketches of roadways from his lesson-plans during his time as a teacher and a selection of his paintings from *The*

Figure 6: *Richard Demarco. La strada, le route, the road*. Museo Nazionale Castello Pandone October 2019. [Courtesy of Cultural Documents.]

Figure 7: Self-portrait by Richard Demarco, 1948.

Road to Miekle Seggie; despite the road being a core element in the collective consciousness of this community, it is extremely rarely addressed. The 1967 image of Demarco and Emilio Coia depicts two sharply-dressed young creatives at the entrance to the Demarco Gallery in Melville Crescent, Edinburgh; their glances, aware of both the camera and each other, evidence their shared heritage and ambitious burgeoning identities.

The vitrines and banners of the final room displayed both Richard's achievements as an established practitioner and also accolades stimulated by his work, concluding with his most recent activities at the heart of the contemporary art world at the Venice Biennale and his return to contextualise his life and work through the imaginary portal which coastal west

facing page:

Figure 8: Sketch of Italian coastal fishermen by Richard Demarco 1950.

Figure 9: Sketchbook page titled *Use of roads to indicate form of the landscape* by Richard Demarco, 1943.

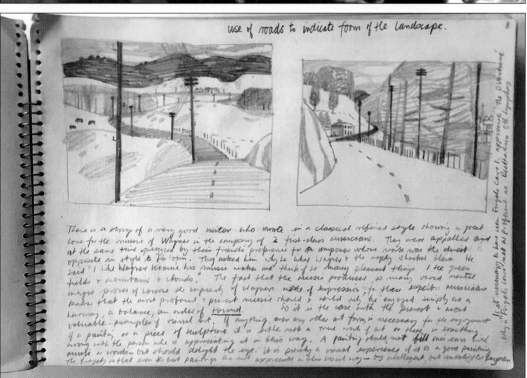

use of roads to indicate form of the landscape.

There is a story of a very good writer who wrote in a classical refined style showing a great love for the music of Wagner in the company of 2 first-class musicians. They were appalled and at the same time puzzled by their friend's preference for a composer whose work was the direct opposite in style to his own. They asked him why he, why Wagner & the rhapsody shocked them. He said "I like Wagner because his music makes me think of so many pleasant things I see green fields & mountains & clouds." The fact that the music produced so many vivid mental images proves of course the impurity of Wagner's mode of expression; to these expert musicians proves that the most profound & purest music should & could only be enjoyed simply as a harmony, a balance, an order of sound. So it is the case with the purest & most valuable examples of visual art. If anything over any other art form is necessary for the enjoyment of a painting or a piece of sculpture it is little less a true work of art or there is something wrong with the person who is appreciating it in this way. A painting should not fill our ears with music or wisdom but should delight the eye. It is purely a visual experience if it is a good painting. The tragedy is that even the best paintings are not appreciated in this visual way — by intelligent but uncultured laymen.

Scotland has represented to him since his evacuation as a ten year old during WWII.

The prescribed route through the exhibition came to an end at a junction between rooms and gave an opportunity to look back towards the beginning of the exhibition, and re-consider its stories, in reverse-order, from the present into the past. This offered visitors, Richard and me an opportunity to reflect again on Richard's ancestry and life in relation to ours. There was a sense of journey and expanded territory, unrestricted by state borders and cultural conventions, and of both consistency and evolution that indicated towards new or 'third' cultures.

La Strada, Le Route, The Road en-abled me to bring specific aspects to the forefront of Richard's attention; how his ancestry of travel had defined his sense of territorial identity; the role his father played in developing his awareness of his entitlement to multiple places and cultures; the extent to which Richard has been affected by the impact of war on the lives of ordinary people; the role models Richard encountered during his youth, and how these aspects have shaped Richard's sense of the possibilities in his work. In turn the sense of enduring professional and personal quest which Richard represents to me endorses my own ongoing work piecing together traces of cultural identities to make my sense of the past and present.

Biographies of the Contributors

Jon Blackwood studied art history at the University of St. Andrews and the Courtauld Institute of Art and has worked subsequently both in the gallery and university sectors. From 2011–14 he lived between Sarajevo, Bosnia and Skopje, Macedonia pursuing research into Yugoslav-era art and contemporary art in the post-Yugoslav republics.

Active as a curator and researcher, Jon has written books including *Critical Art in Contemporary Macedonia* (mala galerija, Skopje, 2016) and contributed essays to edited collections such as *Art & Activism in an Age of Systemic Crisis* (edited Steinbock, Ieven & de Valck, Routledge, New York & London, 2020), and *EWVA: European Womens' Video Art in the Seventies and Eighties* (edited Leuzzi, Shemilt & Partridge, John Libbey, 2019). His writings have also appeared in *a-n* and *Art Monthly*.

Jon's past exhibitions include *Property of Emptiness* (Institute of Contemporary Art, Zagreb 2015), *Captured State: New Art from Macedonia* (Summerhall, Edinburgh, 2017), *Utopian Realism: Mladen Miljanoviæ* (Peacock Visual Arts, Aberdeen, 2019), *Overcoming Art* (SCS Jadro, Skopje 2021) and *Nothing's Guaranteed: Exhibition of Bosno-Futurism* (Summerhall, Edinburgh 2022).

Jon is currently a reader in contemporary art at Gray's School of Art, Robert Gordon University, Aberdeen and divides his time between Aberdeen, Sarajevo and Skopje.

Gabriella Cardazzo is a Venetian scholar, contemporary art curator, director, documentary filmmaker and video maker.

She directed the historic Galleria del Cavallino for 24 years, with her brother Paolo, and after that, she founded the organisation ArtSpace. She has been collaborating with Trieste Contemporanea for many years, contributing with focus on 20th Century Contemporary culture authors from Eastern Europe as well as on topics of multidisciplinary relevance (including the programme on Tadeusz Kantor in 2010, Stanisław Ignacy Witkiewicz in 2013, the exhibition *A la frontière* in 2016, the exhibition *La ricerca dell'identità (al tempo del selfie)* in 2019, and the exhibitions on Paul Neagu and on Malgorzata Dmitruk in 2021).

Dr. Cav. **Terri Colpi** is an Honorary Research fellow at the University of St Andrews. A third generation Scottish Italian by birth, she has lived in the countryside on the Hampshire-Sussex border for almost thirty years.

After obtaining her doctorate at the University of Oxford, researching Italian migration to Bedford, she worked for five years at the Italian Consulate General in London. Combining her knowledge of Italians in Scotland, her work on Bedford and her insights into the London Italian presence, her first two books, published in 1991 still form the starting point for research in this field, an area that has steadily expanded since then and one across which Terri Colpi has maintained a leading role. Awarded the honour of *Cavaliere,* Knight of the Italian Republic, for her contribution and recognised internationally as a pre-eminent authority on Italian migration to the UK, she has published widely, presented papers at many conferences in this country, Italy and elsewhere, given public lectures in Edinburgh, Glasgow and London, participated in media collaborations with Sky Arts, the BBC and CNN and continues to be active within 'Italian Britain'. For example, at London's Italian Cultural Institute she co-organised a conference on the Arandora Star in November 2021, bringing together for the first time academics, politicians and MPs from both Italy and the UK, British Italian celebrities and members of the Italian communities.

As a consummate lover of Italy, Italians and Italian culture, it is no coincidence that Terri Colpi's arboretum in Hampshire, her other passion, features an historic Italianate garden at its centre. Designed by Arts and Crafts landscape architect Inigo Triggs, who had strong connections to Italy and especially Sicily, it highlights symmetry, fountains and terraces. In 1995, Richard Demarco's 'Garden Route to the Edinburgh Festival', encompassing some thirty gardens and following a path northward from Italy and Belarus through England and Scotland, alighted at Terri Colpi's garden. A memorable day of poetry, performance and communion with the natural world embraced her fusion of 'natura e cultura' reinforcing dialogue with Demarco and characterising a friendship that acknowledges a shared heritage.

Francesca Gallo teaches Contemporary Art History at Sapienza University of Rome and has written several essays and articles on *Les Immatériaux* (Centre Pompidou 1985) and on Jean-François Lyotard. Lately, her research has focused on Italian neo-vanguards with a focus on Ketty La Rocca (Postmediabooks 2015; Biennale Donna 2018), Giuseppe Chiari (Giunti 2019; *Il Capitale Culturale* 2020), video art (Mimesis 2018 and *L'Uomo nero* 2018) and performance (*Ricerche di storia dell'arte* 2014 e *Modern Italy* 2021). Her interest in performance was developed in her book *Parole, voci, corpi tra arte concettuale e performance. Conferenze, discussioni, lezioni come pratiche artistiche in Italia* (2022), the first systematic study on the discursive approaches to live action from the 70s to date. Recently, she edited, among the others, *Artiste italiane e immagini in movimento. Identità, sguardi, sperimentazioni* (with L. Conte, 2021) and *Anticolonialismo e postcolonialismo nelle arti visive: prospettive italiane*, "From the European South", (6/2020). From her research in the Mara Coccia Archive, she curated an exhibition at Galleria Nazionale of Rome (2020, exhibition catalogue Silvana) and wrote several contributions, among which a chapter for the comprehensive book

Women Art Dealers, currently under publication by Bloomsbury.

Marco Maria Gazzano (1954–2022) was an expert in film, electronic arts and intermedialities. He was Associate Professor of Film, Photography and Television in the Faculty of Literature and Philosophy at the Università degli Studi Roma Tre. He taught *Film Theory* and *Cinema, Electronic Arts and Intermediality* and organised and directed several international conferences from 2003 to his death.

From 1984 he taught in different universities in Italy and Europe and took part in the design and making of experimental broadcast programming in collaboration with RAI – Italian Radio and Television and TSI – Italian Swiss Television.

From 1984 to 1996 he was the Director of the *Locarno VideoArt Festival* (CH) and from 1997 to 2001 of the *Art & Communication International Biennale of Electronic Arts, Quality Television & Multimedia Publishing Trade* in Rome. He also curated solo exhibitions of many artists including Nam June Paik, Steina and Woody Vasulka, Robert Cahen, Gianni Toti, Mario Sasso, Adriana Amodei, Ida Gerosa, Federica Marangoni, Alba D'Urbano, Marianne Strapatsakis, Carlo Quartucci, Carla Tatò, and Edison Studio in Europe.

In 1989 he founded and became President of the Cultural Association, *Kinema* in Rome.

He was the creator of numerous academic projects and of the international exhibition project *Tower of Peace. The strategies of the art strategies against violence* (2002–2013) and creator of the European satellite TV channel *ArsTv Network*.

He was a Member of the Academic Board of the Ph.D. "Landscapes of the contemporary city. Political, technical and visual studies" at University of Roma Tre; and directed the book series *Immagini in movimento* (Exorma, Roma) and was member of the editorial boards of several journals including *Cinema Nuovo*, *Praxis*, and *Imago Film & Media Studies* (Università degli Studi Roma Tre / Sapienza University of Rome). He also edited special issues of *Bianco e Nero*, the historic journal of the Experimental film centre in Rome.

In 2012 he edited the monography of his theoretical essays from 1976, *Kinema*.

Il cinema sulle tracce del cinema. Dal film alle arti elettroniche, andata e ritorno (Exorma, Roma 2012, 2014) – *Kinema. From film to electronic arts*.

Laura Leuzzi is an art historian and curator. Dr Leuzzi was Research Fellow and Co-Investigator on the AHRC funded project *Richard Demarco: The Italian Connection* (2018–2021; DJCAD, University of Dundee). She was Postdoctoral researcher on the AHRC funded projects *EWVA - European Women's Video Art in the 70s and 80s* (2015-2018) and *REWINDItalia Artists' Video in Italy in 70s and 80s* (2011–2014), both at DJCAD. She is the author of articles and essays in books and exhibition catalogues, with her research focused on early video art, European video art histories, art and feminism, activism and new media. She has presented internationally and given lectures at several universities. She is co-editor of *REWINDItalia. Early Video Art in Italy* (John Libbey, 2015) and *EWVA European Women's Video Art in the 70s and 80s* (John Libbey 2019). She is currently Honourary Visiting Research Fellow at Gray's School of Art, RGU, and University of Abertay and Researcher at Sapienza University of Rome.

Adam Lockhart is a Lecturer and Researcher in Media Art & Archives at Duncan of Jordanstone College of Art & Design (DJCAD) at the University of Dundee. His research is rooted in the creative economies of cultural assets and how they can be unlocked to influence and affect wider society. He manages the DJCAD media archives which include the collections of the Demarco Digital Archive, REWIND | Artists' Video, REWIND*Italia*, European Women's Video Art (EWVA) and the Alastair MacLennan performance archive. He has worked on many funded research projects including *REWIND | British Artists' Video in the 70s & 80s*, *Narrative Exploration in Expanded Cinema* with Central St Martins College of Art & Design, REWIND*Italia*, *EWVA, Alastair MacLennan: Beyond the Archive* and *Richard Demarco: The Italian Connection*. He is part of the strategic working group for the future of the Demarco Archives, having worked with Richard Demarco since 2005. Lockhart is an established leading specialist and researcher in the conservation, preservation, restoration and re-exhibition of artists' moving image, working with artists, galleries and archives and manages the specialist DJCAD Media Preservation Lab. He has acted as an advisor for the sale of artworks to national museums by artists such as David Hall, Stephen Partridge and Tina Keane. Lockhart has acted as curator, co-curator and consultant for a number of screenings and exhibitions at places such as Tate Modern, Tate Britain, BFI Southbank, Dundee Contemporary Arts, Scottish National Galleries of Modern Art, Stills Edinburgh, Streetlevel Photoworks Glasgow, DOCVA in Milan and Shanghai Minsheng Art Museum. He has written for numerous publications and lectured widely. As an artist, he produces and performs music/sound for avant-garde projects, live cinema soundtracks and alternative music. He also creates video artworks and installations making use of archive material, responding to archives through re-interpretation and manipulation.

Dr **Deirdre MacKenna** PhD is a programmer, curator, producer, teacher/lecturer and assessor/evaluator of visual art programmes and projects. Her heritage in the west Scotland, France, Ireland and Italy is an important aspect of her work.

Her doctoral thesis 'Sensemaking through durational engagement with cultural programming' (2019) elaborated how culture-production can give voice to underrepresented communities.

After her roles as inaugural Exhibitions Curator of University of Dundee (1994–2001) and Director of Stills, Edinburgh (2002–2014), she founded the nonprofit agency *Cultural Documents* which initiates partnerships to reify and activate engagement around intangible aspects of society, rural/coastal places and the environment.

Cultural Documents has generated a wide range of thematic cultural programmes, research, commissions, artworks, touring-exhibitions, events, presentations, lectures, lesson-plans and publications through collaborations with individuals, independent collective groups, international diasporic communities and institutions. www.culturaldocuments.net

Terry Ann Newman was born in Wiltshire in 1944 and educated in Southampton, gaining a Diploma in Fine Art from the College of Art in 1987. Since meeting Richard Demarco in 1983, she has travelled extensively in Europe, particularly in Eastern Europe during the 1980s and 90s with the Demarco Gallery's 'Edinburgh Arts'; she has been a director of the Demarco European Art Foundation since 1992, and deputy to Richard Demarco since 2000. Her art works are in private and public collections, including the National Galleries of Lithuania and Hungary.

Stephen Partridge is an artist and academic researcher (PI/CI on the AHRC-funded video art archival and historical projects REWIND, Expanded Cinema, Rewind*Italia, European Women's Video Art* and *Richard Demarco | The Italian Connection*). He was in the landmark video shows of the 1970s including *The Video Show* at the Serpentine in 1975, *The Installation Show* at the Tate gallery in 1976, *The Paris Biennalle* in 1977 and a solo exhibition at The Kitchen in New York in 1979. During the eighties he exhibited widely and also became interested in works for broadcast television and was commissioned by Channel 4 television to produce *Dialogue for Two Players* in 1984. With Jane Rigby, he formed Fields and Frames Ltd – an arts projects and television production company – which produced the innovative *Television Interventions* project for Channel 4 in 1990, with nineteen works by artists for television (including his own piece in the series – *The Sounds of These Words*. He also co-produced a short series of student and artists work, *Not Necessarily*, with BBC Scotland for BBC2 network television in 1991. He has also curated a number of influential exhibitions: *Video Art 78* in Coventry; UK TV New York; *National Review of Live Art* 1988-90; 19:4:90 *Television Interventions*; and the touring tape packages *Made in Scotland I, II, Semblances, Passages, and David Hall: Situations Envisaged* at the Richard Saltoun Gallery in London in 2015. He lectured from 1975- 2019 in a number of art colleges, and established the School of Television & Imaging at Duncan of Jordanstone College of Art & Design (University of Dundee) where he was Dean of Research from 2001–2019. He is currently Professor Emeritus with the Transtechnology Research Group at the University of Plymouth. His seminal work *Monitor* (1974) was acquired by TATE in December 2014.

Elaine Shemilt is an academic, researcher, and practising artist and was the Chair of Fine Art Printmaking at DJCAD, University of Dundee (2001–2021). Elaine is especially known as a printmaker and was a pioneer of early feminist video and multi-media installation. She continues to address the impact of war, conflict, censorship and constraint on psychologies and environments in her work. She is P.I. on the AHRC-funded research projects: EWVA, investigating early video art by European women artists; and Demarco | The Italian Connection. She is the Director of the *Centre for Remote Environments* – a research and consultancy unit for environmental projects, mainly concerned with the Island of South Georgia for which she was made a Shackleton Scholar in 2001.

Her artistic practice involves sculpture, installation, printmaking, video and digital media. She has experimented with a combination of materials and media and earned an international reputation for innovation in the use of printmaking across art forms and her collaborative work with scientists. Shemilt is a graduate of Winchester School of Art and the Royal College of Art, and has exhibited internationally including the Hayward Gallery, Imperial War Museum, ICA London, Edinburgh International Festival, MACRO Roma, Bibliotheque Nationale de France and at Casa Goldoni Museum, Venice. Since 2018 her work has been acquired and is touring within the exhibition *Feminist Avant-Garde of the 1970s* from the SAMMLUNG VERBUND Collection.

Index

Selected Bibliography

D. Bellman (ed.), *A Journey from Hagar Qim to the Ring of Brodgar*, Richard Demarco Gallery, Edinburgh 1976.

S. T. Buckle, 'Is this the Face of Alessandro di Marco? The Forgotten Features of a Well-Known Italian Model', *The British Art Journal*, 13.2 (2012), 67-75.

M. Calvesi, Le due avanguardie [Milan: Lerici Editore, Milano, 1966, Laterza, Bari-Roma 1998.

T. Colpi, 'Chaff in the Winds of War? The Arandora Star, Not Forgetting and Commemoration at the 80th Anniversary', *Italian Studies*, 75.4 (2020), 389-410 into the bibliography.

T. Colpi, *Italians' Count in Scotland. Recording History, The 1933 Census*, The St James Press, London 2015.

R. Demarco, *Richard Demarco: A Life in Pictures* (Ellon: Northern Books, 1995.

R. Demarco, *The Road to Meikle Seggie*, Luath Press, Edinburgh 2015.

R. Demarco, *A unique partnership Richard Demarco, Joseph Beuys*, Luath Press, Edinburgh 2016.

R. Demarco (ed.) *Tavola*, exhibition catalogue, Richard Demarco Gallery, Edinburgh 1988.

J. Falconer, Edinburgh Festival catalogue, Edinburgh 1947.

F. Gallo (ed.), *Works and Archives. Mara Coccia*, exhibition catalogue (Rome, 18 June – 20 September 2020), Silvana, Cinisello Balsamo 2020.

L. Leuzzi, 'Edimburgo-Roma 1967, connessioni italo-scozzesi sulle tracce della mostra *Contemporary Italian Art* alla Richard Demarco Gallery', *Storia dell'arte*, 2019, n. 1-2, pp. 205-215.

L. Leuzzi, 'Il talento e la sorte. Il talento e la sorte. La liaison Edimburgo-Venezia dell'Italian Connection di Richard Demarco', *Engramma*, n. 162, 2019.

L. R. Lippard, *Overlay Contemporary Art and the Art of Prehistory*, The New Press, New York 1983.

E. McArthur & A. Watson (eds.), *10 Dialogues. Richard Demarco, Scotland and the European Avant Garde,* Royal Scottish Academy of Art and Architecture, Edinburgh 2010.

C. Ricci (ed.), *Starting From Venice*, EtAl, Milan 2010.

Roma Punto Uno, exhibition catalogue, with a text by M. Carboni, Leader Offset, Perugia 1989

M. Santulli, *Modelle e Modelli Ciociari nell'Arte Europea, a Roma, Parigi, Londra nel 1800-1900,* Edizione Ciociaria Sconosciuta, Arpino 2010.

G. Sutherland, *On the Road to Meikle Seggie. Richard Demarco's Edinburgh Arts Journeys 1972-80*, PhD Thesis, University of Dundee, 2020.

To Callanish From Hagar Qim, with an introduction by L. Lippard, The Richard Demarco Gallery, Edinburgh 1975.

A. Watson (ed.), *Demarco 2020*, Demarco Archive Trust, Edinburgh 2021.